PUBLIC POLICY

Origins, Practice, and Analysis

Kimberly Martin | Keith E. Lee Jr | John Powell Hall

UNG

UNIVERSITY of
NORTH GEORGIA™
UNIVERSITY PRESS

Blue Ridge | Cumming | Dahlonega | Gainesville | Oconee

ISBN: 978-1-940771-83-0

Produced by:
University System of Georgia

Published by:
University of North Georgia Press
Dahlonega, Georgia

Cover Design and Layout Design:
Corey Parson

For more information, please visit http://ung.edu/university-press
Or email ungpress@ung.edu
Instructor Resources available upon request.

TABLE OF CONTENTS

CHAPTER 3: FOUNDATIONS OF THE POLICY PROCESS   35

CHAPTER 4: PROBLEM IDENTIFICATION AND AGENDA SETTING 53

CHAPTER 5: POLICY DESIGN AND FORMULATION   80

Acknowledgments

The authors would like to thank their families for their tolerance and understanding during the writing and editing process. We'd also like to thank the graduate mentors and colleagues who have educated and inspired us throughout the years. Finally, the authors thank Yinning Zhang for her tireless and persistent guidance. This project might never have been completed without her thoughtful attention to detail and patience during a pandemic.

1

Introduction to Public Policy

1.1 CHAPTER OBJECTIVES:

- Introduce and define public policy.
- Differentiate between policy and politics.
- Recognize why and how students should study public policy.
- Identify various types of public policies.
- Outline the Plan of the Book.

1.2 WHAT IS PUBLIC POLICY?

What is the most pressing problem facing the American public today? Is it immigration reform, health care costs, the student debt crisis, stagnating wages, or a budget deficit reaching into the trillions? How about climate change or the threat of plastic pollution in the ocean? What about gun violence and gun rights? The problems facing the U.S. are numerous, but solutions exist, and it is within the power of government to provide those solutions by developing thoughtful and effective public policy.

We know that *public* refers to the people, and American government was established to serve at the will of the people. Unlike the word "public's" precise definition, **public policy** has numerous ways to be defined and just as many opinions about what it entails. Table 1.1 provides definitions for public policy from some of the leading textbooks on this topic.

Definitions of Public Policy in Various Texts

Definition	Author
"Public policy is the outcome of the struggle in government over who gets what."	Clark Cochran et al. 2010
"Stated most simply, public policy is the sum of government activities, whether acting directly or through agents, as it has an influence on the life of citizens."	B. Guy Peters 2010
"Whatever governments choose to do or not to do."	Thomas Dye 2013
"A statement by government—at whatever level, in whatever form—of what it intends to do about a public problem."	Thomas Birkland 2019
"A course of action adopted by the government in response to public problems."	Rinfret, Scheberle, and Pautz 2019

Table 1.1: Definitions of public policy in various texts.
Source: Original Work
Attribution: K.Martin, inspired by table in Thomas Birkland (2019).
License: CC BY-SA 4.0

While it would be impossible to agree on one definition, common themes exist throughout the literature. First, public policy is created by the government, and private business activity is not included in its definition. For instance, popular social networking websites, owned by private entities, can make it their policy to prohibit specific individuals (suspected terrorists, hate groups, criminals) from using their platforms. This practice is not truly public policy since it does not originate from the government. There are, however, instances in which public policy and private sector policy intersect. Notably, Apple has consistently refused to unlock iPhones owned by terrorist suspects for the FBI (Collier and Farivar, 2020). The Department of Justice and the tech industry have argued for decades about the tradeoffs between privacy and national security. In most cases, the FBI has been able to unlock iPhones without help from Apple, but the government continues to apply pressure to Apple, hoping they will change the policy.

Second, public policy occurs as a response to a public problem. Public problems are issues that the government has the power to resolve. It is important to note that while the government might have the power to resolve public problems, the government faces many problems it has yet to resolve, such as drug addiction, poverty, or homelessness. Shrimping nets exemplify a problem that government was able to resolve. Shrimping nets are a threat to sea turtles that get caught in the mesh and drown. In response, the National Marine Fisheries Service requires shrimp fishers to use turtle excluder devices that allow turtles to escape if they are caught (NOAA). These turtle excluder devices exemplify public policy formulated specifically to solve a public problem.

Figure 1.1: Turtle escaping a net with a turtle excluder device.
Source: NOAA Fisheries
Attribution: NOAA Fisheries
License: Public Domain

If a state governor develops a program that encourages schools to offer healthy food items on their lunch menu, this initiative is also a public policy. However, if a senator from Georgia opposes same-sex marriage, their doing so is not an example of public policy. The senator is entitled to their opinion, but the Defense of Marriage Act (DOMA) in 1996 and the Supreme Court's ruling in *Obergefell v. Hodges* (2015) both address same-sex marriage. These government resolutions are considered public policy. DOMA is an example of legislative policy making. Congress has wide-ranging power to create public policy; in fact, it is the primary responsibility of the legislative branch. *Obergefell v. Hodges* (2015) is an example of judicial policy making. While many scholars argue that the courts should not have the power to make public policy, the court's rulings often result in the development of new policy or changes to existing policy. Congress and the court's role in the policy making process will be addressed in more depth throughout this text.

1.3 WHY STUDY PUBLIC POLICY?

Many students do not realize how much public policy affects them on a daily basis. If you are a college student, you may wake up in a dorm funded by a federal program. You might put on clothing made in China or India and subject to import tariffs and regulations. In the dining hall, you may have breakfast cereal and milk regulated by the Food and Drug Administration. The Federal Communications

Commission regulates the network that your phone operates on. You check your email using the internet, which was developed with federal funding. Later in the day, you may drive to the grocery store to pick up snacks in a car designed according to federal guidelines. That same evening, you may have some friends over and decide to do something crazy like get matching tattoos! Safety standards for the tattoo parlor and tattoo artists are also regulated by state government. Almost everything you experience throughout your daily life is touched by government action in some way. Why, then, study public policy? With so much at stake, the more appropriate question is who would *not* want to play a role in, or at least become more knowledgeable about, the policy process?

Rinfret, Scheberle, and Pautz (2019) write that understanding the policy process is essential for individuals because familiarity with the system allows us to effectively address problems in our community. Students studying public policy will quickly learn that multiple people and institutions are involved in the policy making process and many opportunities exist for citizens to play a direct role. Furthermore, increasing the number of citizens who understand the policy making process will lead to better solutions to public problems. Studying public policy will help you learn to become a more active participant in our government so that your voice can be heard during policy debates. Most importantly, if we do not participate in these discussions we may end up living with policies we do not support.

An interest in public policy could also lead to a lucrative career in the field. Policy professionals come from a variety of disciplines and backgrounds, from health care and education to economic and foreign policy. These practitioners are experts in their fields and have the ability to influence public policy in profound ways. Indeed, the prospect of directly influencing public policy without ever seeking elected office has definite allure.

Regardless of your career ambitions, you will certainly find yourself involved in politics or public policy at some point in your life. Eventually a mall in your town could be abandoned, leading citizens and the city council to come together to address the blighted and vacant property. One day you may face community concerns regarding overdevelopment or contaminated water sources. At some point, you may see a spike in crime rates in your neighborhood. Perhaps your neighbor is deported, or your child is unable to receive a necessary surgery because of health care costs. Such situations will spur you to suddenly recall the lessons learned in this course and realize that you have the power as a citizen to influence public policy.

1.4 HOW TO STUDY PUBLIC POLICY

Public policy involves much more than understanding politics and political institutions, like Congress, the President, the Supreme Court, interest groups, etc. Problems and the search for solutions drive policy studies. Certainly, elections are exciting and easily catch the public's attention due to the intense focus media gives them. However, what comes after the election, that is, public policy, is fascinating in its own right. The policy process is complicated and exciting, particularly in an environment like our current political climate, where nothing is black and white.

When studying politics and government institutions, political scientists often pursue knowledge using "pure" theoretical science, meaning their research stems from broad, abstract ideas. While the study of public policy follows a similar path, public policy research is often practical or applied in nature. For example, recently published articles in the *Journal of Policy Analysis and Management* focus on practical subjects, such as how to make immigration reform policies more efficient (Bean, 2019) or how to utilize housing vouchers to improve academic performance for high school students (Schwartz et al., 2019). As Birkland writes, "The practical and applied study of public policy takes its cues from theory, but seeks more actively to apply those theoretical insights to actual cases of public policy formation" (Birkland, 2019, p. 19). In a course on public policy, students may be asked to apply theoretical concepts to a practical case. For example, John Kingdon's Multiple Streams framework (chapter 4) seeks to explain why some policies are successful and others are not, and can be applied to a number of policies, including immigration, education, and health care. In fact, many policymakers use theoretical insights while attempting to get their ideas passed, even if they may not realize that particular goal.

> **Stop and Think**
>
> What are your plans post-graduation? In what ways might you be involved in politics or public policy?

Students of public policy can expect early exposure to theoretical concepts. These concepts will then be applied to real world cases to better understand and solve public problems. Undoubtedly, there are many applied political science studies, but students of public policy learn a different skill set, one that encourages them to identify problems, develop solutions, and evaluate proposed policies as well as those already put into practice.

1.5 TYPES OF PUBLIC POLICY

Public policy is all around us, but the policies developed by lawmakers come in many different forms. Some policies distribute a good or service to everyone. Others seek to redistribute benefits and foster equality for certain groups. Finally, some intend to regulate behaviors and establish executive agencies. The term **government actors** is comprehensive and refers to any person acting on behalf of the government. This term will be used throughout the text when discussing government workers at the federal, state, and local levels. To that end, public policy can be made by government actors at all levels of government. Thomas Lowi argued that policy can be classified into four categories: distributive, redistributive, regulatory, and constituent policies (Lowi, 1964). Even today these classifications continue to adequately describe most government policies (Collie, 1988).

1.5.1 Distributive Policies

Distributive policies allow government actors to provide beneficial goods and services to a majority of the population at the expense of all taxpayers. They are designed to improve the equitable distribution of goods and services by providing benefits to a large portion of the population rather than by taking from one group and giving to another (Peters et al., 1977). Two realities of distributive policies make them the least controversial form of government policy: everyone shares their benefits, and the general public pays their costs (Weingast, 1994).

Distributive policies are easy to recognize and policy goals are typically easy to identify. The public encounters distributive policies every day. Examples include public roads and public education. Public highways are paid for by all taxpayers and built by government agencies for the good of the whole population. Public transportation infrastructure, funded by taxpayers, serves to benefit all groups within society. The same can be said for public education. Public schools are paid for by all citizens (whether they have children or not) and provide society with a well-educated workforce that further benefits the overall economic growth of the nation.

Figure 1.2: Highway funding is an example of distributive policy.
Source: Wikimedia Commons
Attribution: User "Bamsb900"
License: CC BY-SA 4.0

1.5.2 Redistributive Policies

Redistributive policies reallocate wealth, property, political or civil rights, or some other valuable item to the advantage of class-based groups (Hill and Leighley, 1992, Jongho and Berry, 2008). While these policies often involve economic decisions, they can also involve the redistribution of social status. For instance, redistributive economic policies redistribute income and wealth from the wealthiest population to the poorest. Civil rights policies are intended to provide social benefits to minorities and women so that they may obtain economic and social equality (Peters et al., 1977).

Redistributive policies are more controversial than distributive policies because they provide benefits to specific groups at the expense of others. Federal welfare programs, like the Supplemental Nutrition Assistance Program (SNAP) and Temporary Assistance for Needy Families (TANF), are controversial examples of redistributive public policy programs (Weingast, 1994). Supporters argue that SNAP and TANF provide benefits to Americans in need of economic assistance, while those who oppose these policies see them as taking taxpayer money from the working class and redistributing funds to those who are not working.

Despite the ever-present controversy associated with redistributive policies they are frequently utilized when policymakers perceive that economic growth is not evenly distributed. Minimum wage laws have redistributive qualities and will continue to be debated at the state and federal government levels for years to come. Supporters argue that increasing the minimum wage to $15 an hour will generate higher levels of equality in the distribution of earnings, leading to a reduction in poverty. Those opposed to minimum wage increases argue that such a law would actually increase poverty due to a reduction in hours worked and fewer employment opportunities (Bourguignon, 2018).

1.5.3 Regulatory Policies

One of the most important services provided by the government is the protection of individual rights which are necessary for the establishment of law and order in any civilization. **Regulatory policies** allow the government to compel certain beneficial behaviors from individuals or groups while discouraging other behaviors. Government regulatory policies involve the implementation of rules by government actors, rules that are backed by the law (Brown and Jackson, 1994). Regulatory policies place constraints on unacceptable individual and group behaviors (Peters et al., 1977).

Stop and Think

Give an example of a regulatory policy. If you cannot think of one, research food safety regulations.

The goal of regulatory policies, then, is to provide a safe atmosphere for all individuals without resulting in an excessive loss of rights or freedoms. Prohibitions on driving under the influence of alcohol and limitations on unfair business practices are two examples of regulatory public policies. Government policies limiting the price of electricity and water utilities are another example of regulatory actions. Government licensing requirements for specific professions, safety requirements for pharmaceuticals, limitations on toxic emissions and pollutants from factories, and minimum safety requirements for workers are all examples of regulatory policies. Anti-discrimination laws represent another form of regulatory policy intended to improve the lives of minorities and women.

1.5.4 Constituent Policies

Finally, **constituent policies** involve the creation and regulation of government agencies and can also refer to policies that establish the way a government functions. Constituent policies are structural in that they include the creation of government agencies, usually under the executive branch, that work to enforce **statutory laws** created by Congress. Constituent policies are the government's reaction to external stimuli. For example, after the terrorist attacks on the U.S. on September 11, 2001, President George W. Bush's administration established the Department of Homeland Security to improve the ability of federal and state government agencies to combat domestic threats.

Constituent policies also encompass law enforcement, fiscal policy development, and public sector **bureaucratic** regulation. These policies can be procedural in nature; for example, the Substance Abuse and Mental Health Administration's mission is to reduce drug use and aid Americans struggling with mental illness. In this case, the constituent policy was not the establishment of an agency but establishing the functions of that agency. The definition of constituent policy has expanded from what Lowi (1964) once envisioned to include citizen or interest group-initiated policies (Tolbert, 2002). Rather than constituent policies initiated by Congress or executive branch agencies, Tolbert argues that citizen directed democracy efforts have also created constituent polices.

1.6 PLAN OF THE BOOK AND CASE STUDY INTRODUCTION

Public Policy: Origins, Practice, and Analysis, includes seven chapters that introduce students to public policy and the policy making process. Unlike textbooks that include multiple case studies in each chapter, this text uses one case study that runs throughout the book and does so with the intent of giving sufficient detail to a single case familiar to students: the Affordable Care Act of 2010, otherwise known as Obamacare. This case provides an ideal overview of the policy process, and it is used here to explicate each chapter's respective focus. The case study begins with the history of health policy in the U.S. dating back to the eighteenth century and concludes with an analysis of the status quo, along with three alternatives. The healthcare debate, as we examine in chapter two, is rooted in American political culture's relationship with free market capitalism, tied with a lack of faith in a centralized government's ability to carry out policies efficiently. Nevertheless, presidents since Theodore Roosevelt have pushed for healthcare reform. The story of health care's origins follows the themes discussed in chapter two and include the development of American government institutions and the history of U.S. public policy growth.

After considering the historical evolution of American healthcare, we dive directly into the Affordable Care Act (ACA). Chapter three considers the important actors in crafting and passing legislation, with a special focus on shifts within the Senate that allowed for the passing of the ACA. The Senate provides a major hurdle in the legislative process, since it often requires a filibuster proof majority to enact controversial legislation. President Obama entered office with a fifty-nine-seat Senate majority comprising fifty-seven Democrats and two independents who caucused with the Democratic Party. Senator Arlen Spector (R-PA) switched parties in April 2009, thereby giving Democrats a supermajority. Unfortunately for President Obama, Senator Ted Kennedy (D-MA) died in August the same year, thus putting the legislation in jeopardy. Nevertheless, the legislation ultimately passed.

Figure 1.3: Barack Obama signing the Patient Protection and Affordable Care Act.
Source: Wikimedia Commons
Attribution: Pete Souza
License: Public Domain

Chapter four discusses in detail the legislation's passage, giving emphasis to agenda setting. A policy's success depends largely on how it is framed. Democrats and Republicans alike used the media to promote (Democrats) or denounce (Republicans) the policy. Democrats framed the issue as a means of covering more individuals and of allowing individuals already covered more protections, e.g., preventing insurers from denying coverage to consumers with preexisting conditions. Republicans, on the other hand, executed a campaign that dominated the media's attention, most notably with claims of "death panels" and the lack, or loss, of consumer choice.

Chapter five examines the design and formulation of public policy. President Obama campaigned on a public health insurance option, but its elimination was a concession necessary for getting support from a majority of Congressmembers. Furthermore, President Obama established a coalition of groups and individuals (doctors, insurance companies, pharmaceutical companies, labor unions, and elected officials) to design a policy that would reflect a set of shared principles. The result was a policy that allowed states greater influence on policy implementation, thus addressing the barriers mentioned earlier regarding America's distrust of federal government intervention in state policies.

Chapter six considers the implementation of public policy. The partisan backdrop made policy implementation of the ACA challenging, especially its provision requiring state support. The law mandated Medicaid expansion, a provision that relied on state action, which was challenged in court. The Supreme Court ruled the mandate violated the Tenth Amendment, a major setback for implementation. As of 2020, fourteen states have opted out of Medicaid expansion. As with intergovernmental challenges, the policy also relied on coordination between actors outside the political realm, e.g., private insurers, employers, and consumers. Lastly, successful implementation rested on public support. The public disapproved of the policy until 2017, though many favored specific provisions in the law, including protecting coverage of pregnant women and individuals with pre-existing conditions, prohibiting insurers from charging sick people more, and allowing young people to remain on their parents' insurance until age twenty six.

The case study concludes with an analysis of the Affordable Care Act, beginning with the problems Obamacare was unable to solve—making insurance affordable and expanding Medicaid. Various proposals have been offered as a substitute, which we analyze in detail. Each alternative is systematically assessed using a set of established criteria to determine the preferred policy. Taken together, the six sections of the case study will give students an in-depth look at a policy that remains contentious and will remain a salient issue for the foreseeable future.

1.7 CRITICAL THINKING QUESTIONS – INTRODUCTION TO THE ACA

- In Chapter 1 we discuss how public policy touches our everyday lives. Reflect on current debates in health care. What are some of the health care challenges facing the American public today? Have policymakers developed solutions for any of these problems?

- What type of policy is the ACA? Does it take on the characteristics of more than one type of public policy? Explain.

1.8 CHAPTER SUMMARY

In this chapter, we present several definitions of public policy and discuss the importance of policy making on our everyday lives. Public policy is all around us, but the policies developed by lawmakers come in many different forms. Some policies distribute a good or service to everyone. Others seek to redistribute benefits and foster equality for certain groups. Finally, some are meant to regulate behaviors and establish executive agencies. Public policy can be made by government actors at the federal, state, and local levels. Understanding the policy process is important because knowledge about the system allows citizens to effectively address problems in their community. The field of public policy also offers students many lucrative career choices.

1.9 KEY TERMS

- Bureaucrats
- Constituent policies
- Distributive policies
- Government actors
- Public policy
- Redistributive policies
- Regulatory policies
- Statutory Laws
- Constituent Policies

1.10 RESOURCES

Annenberg Public Policy Center. 2019. "Americans' Civic Knowledge Increases but Still Has a Long Way to Go." Accessed December 12, 2019. https://www.annenbergpublicpolicycenter.org/americans-civics-knowledge-increases-2019-survey/

Bean, Frank D. 2019. "Why the United States Must Renew Opportunities to Achieve The American Dream in Order to Reform Immigration Policy." *Journal of Policy Analysis and Management*. Vol. 39. 1. 274-279.

Birkland, Thomas. 2019. *An Introduction to the Policy Process: Theories, Concepts, and Models of Public Policy Making*. New York, NY: Routledge.

Bourguignon, Francois. 2018. "Spreading the Wealth." *Finance and Development*. Vol. 55. 1.

Brown, C.V., and P.M. Jackson. 1994. *Public Sector Economics*. Oxford. United Kingdom.

Cochran, Clarke, Lawrence Mayer, T.R. Carr, N. Joseph Cayer, and Mark McKenzie. 2010. *American Public Policy: An Introduction*. 10th Edition. Boston, MA: Cengage Wadsworth.

Collie, Melissa. 1988. "The Legislature and Distributive Policy Making in Formal Perspective." *Legislative Studies Quarterly*. Vol. 13. 4. 427-458.

Collier, Kevin, and Cyrus Farivar. "The FBI Cracked Another IPhone But It's Still Not Happy with Apple." *NBC News*. 18 May 2020.

Dye, Thomas. 2013. *Understanding Public Policy*. Boston, MA: Pearson.

Laswell, Harold. 1958. *Politcs: Who Gets What, When, How*. New York: Meridian Books.

Lowi, Theodore. 1964. "American Business, Public Policy, Case-Studies." *World Politics*. Vol. 16. 4. 677-715.

National Oceanic and Atmospheric Administration. n.d. "History of Turtle Excluder Devices." Accessed December 12, 2019. https://www.fisheries.noaa.gov/southeast/bycatch/history-turtle-excluder-devices

Peters, Guy. 2010. *American Public Policy: Promise and Performance*. 8th Edition. Washington, DC: CQ Press.

Peters, B. Guy, John C. Doughtie, and M. Kathleen McCulloch. 1977. "Types of Democratic Systems and Types of Public Policy: An Empirical Examination." *Comparative Politics*. Vol. 9. 3. 327-355.

Rinfret, Sara, Denise Scheberle, Michelle Pautz. 2019. *Public Policy: A Concise Introduction*. Thousand Oaks, CA: CQ Press.

Roh, Jongho, and Frances Berry. 2008. "Modeling the Outcomes of State Abortion Funding Referenda: Morality or Redistributive Policy, or Both" *State Politics & Policy Quarterly. Vol.* 8.1. 66-87.

Samuelson, Paul. "Diagrammatic Exposition of a Theory of Public Expenditure." *Review of Economics and Statistics*. 350-356.

Schwartz, Amy Ellen, Keren Horn, Ingrid Ellen, and Sarah Cordes. 2019. "Do Housing Vouchers Improve Academic Performance? Evidence from New York City." *Journal of Policy Analysis and Management*. Vol. 39. 1. 131-158.

Tolbert, C. J. 2002. "Rethinking Lowi's Constituent Policy: Governance Policy and Direct Democracy." *Environment and Planning C: Government and Policy*. Vol 20. 1. 75–93.

Weingast, Barry. 1994. "Reflections on Distributive Politics and Universalism." *Political Research Quarterly*. Vol. 47. 2. 319-327.

2 Origins and Actors

2.1 CHAPTER OBJECTIVES:

- Describe the effect of federalism on national and state policy making.
- Summarize the evolution of federal and state policy-making power.
- Identify primary actors in the policy making process.

2.2 ORIGINS OF PUBLIC POLICY

The origins of public policy are rooted in the origins of civilization itself. As early as the fourth millennia BCE, ancient Sumerian monarchs were making public policy decisions intended to improve the safety and vitality of their cities. Throughout the majority of civilization's history, authoritarian governments made policy decisions without a great deal of direct input from the overall population. The near-absolute policy making power of hereditary monarchs began to slowly change with charters like the Magna Carta (1215) which placed theoretical limits on the power of the British monarch. The "Age of Revolution" in the late eighteenth century changed popular perceptions concerning the proper role of government policy makers and gave rise to the notion that the government's power should be derived from the consent of the governed. Over the last few centuries, laws governing the public policy making process are being added and spelled out in formal, written constitutions. Constitutions identify and restrain the policy making powers of government actors while dictating the access of non-government actors to the policy making process. This chapter will give a brief overview of the historical origins of public policy in the U.S. and explore the different actors influencing policy decisions.

The U.S. federal government was born out of a necessity to improve the previous ruling system and was created by the leaders of the American Revolution. In their first attempt at permanent, national government, these early revolutionary leaders created a confederate government that erred on the side of local (state) government power. Fearing a repeat of the strong, central government against which they were actively fighting to gain independence, early American leaders ratified the Articles of Confederation in 1781. The lessons learned through the many failures of the Articles of Confederation would inform the framers of the United States Constitution and the new federal system of government they would create to replace the initial confederacy. The U.S. Constitution, written in 1787, created the new federal government and established the foundation for federal government policy making.

2.3 ARTICLES OF CONFEDERATION

The Articles of Confederation were introduced in 1776 as an attempt to create a new, permanent government in the American colonies. By 1781, the Articles had been ratified and had officially become the law of the land (McClain and Tauber, 2016). The framers opted for a **confederate government** where policy making power was placed in the hands of local (state) governments. In a confederate

> **Stop and Think**
>
> Why did the Articles of Confederation make it difficult for a centralized government to make policy?

system, the national government's powers are entirely derived from the sovereign local governments. Fearing a return to the oppressive policies associated with a strong **unitary government**, Americans were reluctant to give too much power to their new central government. While a confederate government was philosophically more comfortable for America's early political leaders, over time it proved inadequate for governing the new, and soon to be growing, nation. The inability of the national government to effectively communicate and successfully pass public policies of interest to the entire nation-state, such as national defense, national transportation infrastructure, and regulation of interstate commerce, made the American confederation a poor long-term choice for national government. What the American democratic experiment needed was a revolutionary new form of government that would combine the advantages of unitary and confederate governments and increase the policy making abilities of the federal government. This new government would be born in Philadelphia in 1787.

2.4 U.S. CONSTITUTION AND FEDERALISM

The problem the framers of the Constitution faced was **power**, that is, the ability to get others to do something they would not otherwise do. How much political power should be given to the government, and where should it be placed? The framers had seen first-hand that too much power in the hands of a central government could lead to tyranny and the abuse of individual liberty. However, not enough political power in the central government could lead to anarchy and the tyranny of the majority, that is, when a majority controls a representative government with no protection for the liberty of minorities. The delicate balance between political power and individual liberty was the principal focus of the delegates at the constitutional convention.

The Constitution created a new relationship between federal and state public policy making responsibilities. As we shall discuss in the next section, the federal government enjoys policy making power over several specifically enumerated areas, while the states reserve all other policy making powers for themselves. **Federalism** represents a combination of unitary and confederate governments. The term federalism could best be described as the power sharing relationship between the U.S. federal government and the individual state governments. The Constitution established a power sharing political system in which the federal government would enjoy significant, sometimes exclusive, power in some policy areas while the state governments would maintain significant control in other policy arenas. The Constitution gave the federal government specific **enumerated powers** deemed necessary for ensuring the security and prosperity of the young republic. In addition, the federal court identified several **implied powers** of the federal government that were not specifically enumerated in the Constitution. State governments were enshrined with **reserved powers**, constituting all other policy making powers not given specifically to the federal government or specifically denied to the states. The federal and state governments share **concurrent powers** involving policy areas of interest to both governments (Table 2.1).

Enumerated Powers (Federal Government):
• Regulate Interstate Commerce • Coin Money • Declare War • Make all laws necessary and proper to carry out all enumerated powers
Concurrent Powers (Federal and State Governments):
• Lay and Collect Taxes • Incur Debt • Make and Enforce Laws • Establish Courts and Charter Corporations
Reserved Powers (State Governments):
• Ratify Amendments to the Constitution • Establish Time, Place, and Manner of National Elections • Wield the Police Power • Wield all Power not Specifically Denied to State Governments or Exclusively Given to the Federal Government

Table 2.1 Enumerated, Concurrent, and Reserved Powers Affecting Public Policy
Source: Original Work
Attribution: John Powell Hall
License: CC BY-SA 4.0

2.5 EVOLUTION OF POLICY MAKING IN THE UNITED STATES

Since the ratification of the U.S. Constitution, the principle source of political discord in America has focused on the proper amount of influence the federal and state governments should have over public policy. Put another way, the primary political argument in American history involves the nature of federalism. The distribution of policy making power between the federal and state governments has been driven by the changing expectations of the American people regarding government services.

From the nation's birth in the late eighteenth century through the 1930s, most Americans did not expect the federal government to provide a great deal of public services. During this period of U.S. history, the state governments were more powerful and influential in most domestic policy areas than was the federal government. The federal government was primarily involved in national policy making activities, like building the nation's transportation infrastructure, providing subsidies for westward expansion, protecting domestic commerce by placing tariffs on imported goods, protecting patents, and providing a common currency. Importantly, very few federal government policies were intended to coerce the American population. In short, the federal government's principle policy responsibilities involved assisting economic growth, not regulating the actions of the American people (Ginsberg et al., 2019).

However, after the Great Depression and World War II, the American republic emerged as an economic and military superpower on the global stage. This new international position of strength, along with hard-learned lessons from the Depression illustrating the need for federal government regulatory policies, changed American expectations regarding the role of the federal government. Post-WWII America witnessed an increase in federal government policy making power that, in many ways, continues to this very day.

Many variables were involved in the growth of federal government policy making responsibilities. In addition to the U.S.'s emergence as a global military power, some of the more important elements involved the increased complexity of the U.S. economy, the economic integration of the global economy, and a movement to protect civil liberties for minority groups and women. In short, as the republic changed, the distribution and use of policy making power in the federal system changed with it. The government's regulation of the economy, development of social safety nets, and the protection of civil rights were driven by a population that sought more government services.

As the nation's economy expanded in the late nineteenth and early twentieth centuries, state governments became increasingly unable to provide services they had made available in the past. For example, in the early decades of the republic, the primarily agrarian economy required minimal guidance from state governments. However, the development of a national economy required national government policies to solve national problems. In the 1870s, technological advancements and the development of natural resources dramatically increased the yields of American farmers. At the same time, a new national network of train tracks was connecting the American heartland with the east and west coasts. Due to a lack of federal government regulations and the inability of state governments to regulate interstate commerce, railroad corporations began charging unusually high rates to transport agricultural commodities to foreign markets. In order to obtain redress for these new economic grievances, American farmers turned to the federal government which responded by creating the Interstate Commerce Commission to better regulate the growing economy. This represents an example of federal government initiated constituent and regulatory policies that protect the American population from the damage caused by natural monopolies, a form of market failure that will be discussed later in the text (Kernell et al., 2018).

2.5.1 The New Deal

Early in the 1930s, the maturing republic once again found itself in need of a strong central government if it wished to continue to survive and prosper. The American economy had proved its ability to grow to previously unexpected heights, but it had failed to ensure the success and prosperity of all Americans. Monopolies, low wages, poor working conditions, consumer debt, unfair trade practices, a struggling agricultural sector, and impure foods were some of the national problems associated with the growing, though unregulated, American economy. Consumer spending slowed in the summer of 1929 and unsold goods began to accumulate, leading to a suspension of factory production. Nevertheless, stock prices continued to rise, and by the fall of 1929, nervous investors began selling, resulting in a stock market crash that crippled the world economy.

The devastating global economic depression of the 1930s provided the necessary political capital for President Franklin Roosevelt (1933-1945) to make dramatic changes in the relationship between the national economy and federal government regulatory policies. The programs he adopted are referred to as the **New Deal**, comprising a series of federal government programs intended to reverse the damages of the Great Depression (Simon et al., 2020).

The complexities of the Great Depression and the New Deal policies prevent a quick summary. However, it is accurate to say that the New Deal dramatically changed the federal government's relationship with state governments, the American people, and the national economy. The federal government-initiated policies attempted to improve the economy by regulating prices, creating jobs, regulating banks, and securing the right of labor to collectively bargain with employers. Federal government policies were created that set a minimum wage and established retirement income through the Social Security Act as well as unemployment compensation when jobs were lost. The Roosevelt administration's decisions on these matters were the beginning of many distributive federal policies aimed at increasing economic equity within the American population (Simon et al., 2020). Overall, the New Deal legislation of the 1930s inaugurated a new era for American federalism in which the federal government gained significantly more policy making powers and assumed a much greater role in many aspects of American life.

2.5.2 The Great Society

The **Great Society** was a series of federal government initiatives during the 1960s and 1970s that increased the federal government's power and allowed it to pass regulatory and social policies resembling the New Deal. Democratic majorities in Congress assisted, and in some cases forced, presidents Kennedy, Johnson, and Nixon to enact federal government programs designed to alleviate social inequalities regarding poverty, health care, education, and housing. These policies included the Civil Rights Act of 1964, the Voting Rights Act, the establishment of Medicaid and Medicare, and the Head Start program for low-income children.

One unique characteristic of the Great Society programs, compared to the New Deal legislation a generation earlier, was the extent that the federal government worked with state and local governments to carry out the new policies. The federal government provided increasingly larger amounts of grants-in-aid, money given to state and local governments by the federal government, to improve transportation infrastructure, inner city living conditions, public education, health care, and racial integration (Kollman 2015). The Great Society programs represented an increase in shared policy making powers between the federal and state governments.

Since the passage of the Great Society programs, the federal government has passed many additional notable policies. President Ronald Reagan initiated the War on Drugs, a set of policies meant to reduce the illegal drug trade. President Clinton signed the North American Free Trade Agreement (NAFTA) in an effort to increase trade between Mexico, the U.S. and Canada. The No Child Left Behind Act was signed in 2002 to improve student performance and direct additional federal funding to low-income schools, although the policy is best known for requiring standardized testing in public schools. The Affordable Care Act, known as Obamacare, was signed in 2010 and is discussed in the running case study at the end of each chapter in this text. Meanwhile, state and local governments continue to pass meaningful policies addressing elections, the environment, public safety, taxes, and other social issues. U.S. policy making at all government levels has resulted in a diverse and influential group of laws and rules that guide almost every aspect of how the American public lives and works.

2.6 ACTORS IN THE POLICY PROCESS

As we shall soon discuss, the policy process involves a variety of actors exercising constitutional policy making power, actors in positions that have evolved over the history of the republic, and actors that are outside of government entirely. This chapter will identify and discuss the constitutional actors involved in the policy process and conclude with a description of non-constitutional actors.

2.7 CONSTITUTIONAL ACTORS

The Constitution created a federal government that could address the policy preferences of different political groups within the new republic by allowing regional populations to be represented in the House, state-wide populations that could be best served in the Senate, and the national population that would be represented by the president. The new federal government's policy making powers were separated into a legislative branch that would "make the laws," an executive branch that would "enforce the laws," and a judiciary that would (eventually) give itself the power to "interpret the laws." These three branches of the new federal government, created by Articles One, Two, and Three, of the Constitution, respectively, represent the constitutional actors in the policy process. Most of the enumerated powers given to these three branches are simultaneously separate from, and connected to, the enumerated powers of the other branches. This structure created a government that sacrificed legislative efficiency in exchange for protection from the growth of tyrannical power. The next few sections will discuss the three federal government branches' policy making responsibilities.

2.7.1 Congress

Article One of the Constitution is the longest and most detailed portion of the entire document. The framers of the new republic intended for Congress to be the epicenter of policy making and gave the legislative branch more policy making powers than the executive and judicial branches combined. Congress would serve as a conduit for both translating and filtering public desires into public policy decisions (Whitman-Cobb, 2020). The long history of popularly-elected legislatures, beholden to local populations, was a significant catalyst for the framers' erring on the side of legislative power in the new federal government. The framers of the Constitution made it clear that the legislative branch was to be the first among the three equal branches. (Mann and Ornstein, 2006).

In addition to representation of constituents within specific geographic districts, Congress is responsible for passing legislation, appropriating all revenue spent by the federal government, and providing oversight of the actions of the executive branch. Creating and passing laws is one of the most important and recognizable policy making powers held by Congress. While the lawmaking process is too complex to fit into a simple summary, it is fair to say that the two chambers of the legislative branch share similar characteristics while also displaying unique institutional personalities. One of the most common features of both chambers of Congress can be found in the committee system used to coordinate the passage of legislative bills. Both chambers use specialized standing committees that focus on specific policy areas to discuss legislation before sending it to the full plenary, that is, all members of the particular group (Table 2.2). Discussing policy areas in specific committees creates a division of labor that allows for the development of policy expertise in Congress.

House of Representatives	Senate
Agriculture	Agriculture, Nutrition, and Forestry
Appropriations	Appropriations
Armed Services	Armed Services
Budget	Budget
Energy and Commerce	Energy and Natural Resources
Judiciary	Judiciary
Rules	Finance
Transportation and Infrastructure	Foreign Relations
Ways and Means	Veterans Affairs

Table 2.2 Examples of Congressional Standing Committees
Source: Original Work
Attribution: John Powell Hall
License: CC BY-SA 4.0

Another policy making power that Congress wields is the power of the purse, which describes congressional power to appropriate all revenue spent by the federal government. Appropriation power allows Congress to define the amount of money to be spent by the executive and judicial branches of government

Stop and Think

Why did the framers of the Constitution place so much policy making power in the legislative branch? Can you think of any contemporary examples of Congress exercising policy making power?

while also influencing how legislative policies are implemented. Congressional power over the appropriation of all public funds is one of the most significant checks the legislative branch enjoys over the other two branches of the federal government (Stith, 1988).

The Constitution requires all revenue-raising bills—those bills that include taxes—to originate in the House of Representatives. In 1974, Congress passed the Budget and Impoundment Control Act allowing the legislature to propose alternatives to the president's budget. Congress created the Congressional Budget Office (CBO) to provide itself with the same level of fiscal expertise found in the executive branch's Office of Management and Budget (which puts together the president's budget proposal for congressional approval). The CBO is a nonpartisan agency that allows Congress to accurately assess expected revenues and expenditures for the federal government. The CBO also provides projections for the likely economic effects of different spending programs and information on the costs of proposed policies (Greenstein, 1995).

Finally, the Constitution requires congressional approval for the creation of all executive branch departments and agencies, also known as constituent policy. Congress has the power to oversee how the executive branch is implementing public policy. Congress uses the appropriations process to annually explore what bureaucratic agencies are doing, inform them of what Congress expects them to do, and funds those activities favorable to Congress, while withholding funding from policy areas not popular to a majority of legislators (Wasserman, 2015).

2.7.2 The President

Article Two of the Constitution enumerated far fewer policy making powers and responsibilities to the American president than Congress received in Article One. Fearing too much power in too few hands, the framers saw the executive branch's potential to become tyrannical. However, Article Two contains several pieces of elastic language that have afforded presidents the opportunity to expand their influence over a number of policies when needed. Wielding "the executive power" and taking care that the laws be "faithfully executed" are two of the more prominent avenues used by American presidents to extend their constitutional influence over public policy. Presidents' control over the federal bureaucracy gives them significant influence over the implementation stage of the policy process. As we shall soon see, the president's constitutional role as the nation's chief diplomat provides them with a significant amount of influence over foreign policy making decisions.

The Constitution vested "executive power" into the president. The ambiguity of this clause prevents it from being precisely defined in all circumstances. Several scholars have suggested that the American president has access to more than the specific enumerated powers identified by Article Two and can legitimately exercise unspecified executive power (Milkis and Nelson, 2016). Originally, executive power was viewed as a means to carry out or execute the laws passed by Congress. Today, however, the president controls a bureaucracy spending almost $5 trillion a year—2020 estimates of the Trump administration's budget proposal—and employing almost 3 million public servants.

Presidents have significant power in the policy making process through their control over federal bureaucratic departments (Table 2.3). **Executive orders** are signed and published directives from the president that manage the operations of the federal government. Through executive orders, presidents are able to establish guidelines for federal agencies that possess the force of law. Executive orders do not require congressional approval and are often challenged in court; however, they remain a powerful tool for presidents who wish to utilize more direct policy making powers.

Executive Branch Cabinet Departments	
1. State Department	9. Health and Human Services
2. Treasury Department	10. Housing and Urban Development
3. Defense Department	11. Transportation
4. Justice Department	12. Energy
5. Interior Department	13. Education
6. Agriculture Department	14. Veterans Affairs
7. Commerce Department	15. Homeland Security
8. Labor Department	

Table 2.3 Executive Branch Cabinet Departments
Source: Original Work
Attribution: John Powell Hall
License: CC BY-SA 4.0

The Constitution also gives the president broad powers in the area of foreign policy making. The president is constitutionally responsible for receiving foreign ambassadors and public ministers. Having the president serve as the exclusive representative of the U.S. government encourages consistent foreign policy that is preferable to having all of the voices of Congress pushing different objectives to the international community. The president also simultaneously serves as the U.S. head of state and head of government. This provides additional consistency in the formulation of national policy decisions (Vile, 2010).

The president shares foreign policy decision-making power with the Senate when dealing with the ratification of international treaties. While the Constitution gives the president the power to conduct foreign relations with other governments and negotiate treaties, a two-thirds supermajority vote in the Senate is required for ratification of treaties. When presidents do not enjoy this supermajority support in the Senate, they will often utilize executive agreements that have the same force of law without requiring Senate approval. However, while executive agreements can be created by current presidents without Senate approval, they can just as easily be unilaterally withdrawn by future administrations (Vile 2010).

The president's policy-making influence over legislation has changed dramatically throughout the history of the republic. The president has constitutional power to recommend legislation to Congress, provide information related to the state of the union, and convene Congress in special sessions. While the annual state of the union address has become a significant tool for the president to influence public policy by appealing to the voting public, convening special sessions of Congress has become less valuable as Congress has become more of a year-round job.

The Budget and Accounting Act of 1921 gave the president formal power to submit budget estimates to Congress. This dramatically increased presidential influence over the budgetary process (O'Brien, 2017). The Office of Management and Budget (OMB) provides the chief executive significant influence over the final budget by providing estimates of each executive department's spending needs. While Congress has the final say over appropriations, it is often difficult for the legislative branch to claim to know more about what the executive departments need than does the executive branch.

Finally, regulatory agencies within the executive branch exercise significant influence over public policy through their rule-making power and by issuing new regulations affecting old legislation. While this bureaucratic power was constrained by Congress' Administrative Procedures Act in 1947, the rule-making power of executive branch agencies gives the president extraordinary control over the implementation of public policies (O'Brien, 2017). Having discussed the two elected branches' impact on the policy process, we will now explore the un-elected judiciary's influence on public policy decisions.

2.7.3 The Courts

Article Three created what the framers considered to be the least dangerous branch of the new federal government. The courts have no explicit policy making powers. The court must rely on the other branches of government, at the state and federal level, to enforce its decisions. In general, the judiciary impacts federal and state policies by issuing opinions on the constitutionality of a variety of government policies (Calvi and Coleman, 2004).

The most significant power enjoyed by the federal court—especially in terms of public policy—was not specifically enumerated in Article Three: the power of **judicial review**. This gives the federal court the power to determine if congressional legislation and presidential actions are constitutional. The court's landmark opinion in *Marbury v. Madison* (1803) initiated the court's power of judicial review. Having the power to determine what is or is not constitutional provides the federal court with significant influence over public policy. The other branches of the federal government are expected to honor the rulings of the federal court. While there are select examples of the other branches of government ignoring judicial opinions, the majority of judicial opinions represent a significant judicial check on the elected branches of the federal government (Van Geel, 2005).

Judicial review also gives the federal court policy-making power over state government actions. While exercising the power of judicial review, the federal court is significantly involved in creating public policy, defining the relationship between the branches of the national government, identifying the constitutional powers of state and federal agencies, shaping the liberties of individuals, and bringing social issues to the attention of government and the general population (Wasserman, 2015).

The court's impact on public policy has evolved over the years. In the first century of its existence, the federal court primarily dealt with the relationship between state and national government powers and the issue of slavery. Post-WWII, the court has focused its attention on the protection of civil liberties for women and minority groups (Vile, 2010). The amount of influence the court exerts over public policy is determined by the degree of activism or restraint employed by the court's justices. **Judicial restraint** describes a belief that the court should not push its views on the other branches of government unless an obvious constitutional violation is involved. Judicial restraint calls for less direct judicial influence on public policy. **Judicial activism** views the court as an active member in the policy-making process.

> **Stop and Think**
>
> Imagine life in America if the federal court did not have the power of judicial review. Identify policies that have been ruled unconstitutional by the Supreme Court. How would life in the U.S. be different without judicial review?

Advocates of judicial activism believe the court should use its authority to solve policy problems that have been ignored by the elected branches of government (Wasserman, 2015).

2.8 NON-CONSTITUTIONAL ACTORS: THE BUREAUCRACY

The term bureaucracy refers to the non-elected professionals in government who are responsible for carrying out government policies. Bureaucrats in government are, by definition, influential in the policy process, due to their policy implementation responsibilities. Max Weber (1922) provided the best-known description of the bureaucratic model by identifying six characteristics of public bureaucracies: specialization and identifiable divisions of labor, organizational hierarchy, formal rules governing actions, maintenance of formal records, impersonality, and professionalism based on merit-based hiring practices (Bond and Smith, 2016).

After a series of civil service reforms during and after the Progressive Era, the federal bureaucracy became a more professional organization designed to influence and implement public policy. Over time, a more technically proficient federal bureaucracy went beyond carrying out public policy to interpreting laws and influencing the final policy products. Federal bureaucrats are also significantly involved in the formation of new public policies. The accumulation of policy expertise in the merit-based bureaucracy creates a system where non-elected bureaucrats know more about specific policy areas than do elected officials passing legislation. Contemporary federal bureaucrats have the knowledge required to introduce policy directives and influence the passage of new laws they will be responsible for executing on a daily basis (Whitman-Cobb, 2020).

Bureaucrats are usually most influential during the policy implementation stage of the public policy process. New policies introduced by the legislative branch are generally vague, so they require policy experts within the bureaucracy to implement specific rules governing individual situations. Bureaucrats are also called upon to interpret the meaning of the flexible language used in legislation in order to put specific policies into actual practice. An example of this explication occurred with the Patient Protection and Affordable Care Act (ACA) of 2010. The final version of the ACA legislation was almost 1,000 pages in length, while the subsequent bureaucratic rules attached to it were over 20,000 pages long (Whitman-Cobb, 2020).

Another advantage of the bureaucracy's influence over the policy process is that bureaucrats are usually both informed and accountable. The specialized knowledge accumulated by career bureaucrats in government agencies gives them a unique ability to understand which public policy options are best for the public. This expertise gives them an advantage over elected political leaders responsible for making policy decisions in areas with which_they may not be overwhelmingly familiar. The accountability of public bureaucrats to public institutions can make bureaucratic policy decisions superior to recommendations from interest groups that are not beholden to legitimate sources of authority (Goodsell, 1983). We will now examine the impact of the general population on policy making.

2.8.1 Citizens

Voting is one of the most effective ways for the public to exercise its political power over the elected branches of government. Voting allows citizens to have a direct impact on the policy process by installing elected leaders into office who align with citizen policy preferences. Aside from voting, citizens have many opportunities to influence the policy process. Public opinion is especially influential in a liberal democracy like the U.S. A general understanding of democratic theory suggests that representative government will provide, within reason, what the public demands. While several exceptions exist when the public is passionate and united about an issue, elected leaders tend to make policy decisions in line with public opinion. Policy areas showing high levels of opinion-policy congruence indicate the potentially significant influence of the public on public policy decisions (Bardes and Oldendick, 2012). Such congruence occurs, for example, in a state where the majority of the population favors the death penalty and the state government creates policies that allow for capital punishment.

The general population can also influence public policy decisions by taking direct action. Protections in the First Amendment allow Americans to speak and publish their political opinions, directly address grievances to elected government, and peacefully assemble in order to affect policy decisions. Civic activism, marches, and public protests against unpopular public policies have successfully influenced policy decisions throughout American history. For example, members of the civil rights movement, led by Dr. Martin Luther King Jr., marched on Washington D.C. in 1963 to bring the public's attention to the racial inequalities existing in America. Coupled with protests earlier that year in Birmingham, Alabama, growing public pressure influenced Congress to pass the Civil Rights Act of 1964 the next year. While not constitutionally protected, civil disobedience has also been used to successfully achieve policy goals protecting minority and women's rights (Simon et al., 2020). In the next section, we will discuss the ability of policy makers to be influenced by the actions of interest groups.

2.8.2 Interest Groups

Interest groups influence public policy decisions that favor a specific population. Interest groups are especially powerful in the U.S. due to the constitutional protections afforded to free expression and their ability to have direct contact in representative government. Scholars argue that multiple interest groups clashing over different issues furthers the public good better than any other system (Dahl, 1961). According to this argument, multiple factions (large and small) competing in an open forum to advance their specific causes, create fertile ground for vibrant policy formulation. This argument is known as pluralist theory and will be discussed in greater detail in chapter three.

Interest groups affect public policy in the U.S. in several ways. First, lobbying_is one of the most recognizable methods used by interest groups to promote government action advantageous to their goals. Lobbying is any attempt by interested individuals or groups to influence the votes of policy makers. Generally, lobbyists meet directly with lawmakers to discuss policy preferences, but lobbying can take the form of campaign contributions or other gifts. Recent court decisions equating money spent on political campaigns with First Amendment speech, which is constitutionally protected, have reduced limitations on campaign contributions. This development has increased the influence interest groups have on elected leaders who must raise money for election expenses (total campaign spending in the 2016 election cycle approached $7 billion).

While campaign contributions are an important way interest groups influence legislative decision makers in the policy process, many interest groups do not have the disposable income to invest in elections or direct lobbying. In these cases, the policy-specific expertise developed by interest groups over time often makes information their most valuable commodity. For instance, the U.S. Chamber of Commerce spent the most money on lobbying in 2019 ($77 million). The Chamber is powerful, but compare this level of influence to the exceptionally dominant National Rifle Association (NRA) which spent only $3 million during that same time frame. Lastly, we will briefly discuss the impact of the media on the policy making process.

2.8.3 The Media

The media's influence on policy decisions is also protected by the First Amendment. While the framers of the Constitution disagreed on many policy areas, the protection of open and free expression was one area that enjoyed their near-unanimous support. The marketplace of ideas was viewed as an instrumental piece of the democratic puzzle that deserved special constitutional protections. The free exchange of ideas in public is important for the health of any democratic government because the people must be able to express individual opinions and be knowledgeable and informed when they make political choices. The American media still thrives in this extraordinarily protected area of the U.S. democratic experiment (Bond and Smith, 2016).

The media impacts public policy in several ways. One of the most important involves the media's role in educating the populace. The media serves the public by providing information on what representatives in government are doing. Due to the understandably biased information provided by political candidates and parties, many voters rely on the media to provide a theoretically nonpartisan view of government policy. The independent media also serves a watchdog function by bringing to the public's attention any harmful government actions. For example, in 1971, the *New York Times* published a classified Defense Department study detailing the history of U.S. policy in the Vietnam War. What became known as the "Pentagon Papers" raised public awareness of the difficulties of securing victory in Southeast Asia and increased demand to end combat activities.

The media also influences public policy by determining what issues are covered. This function of the media is called agenda setting, which will be discussed in greater detail in chapter four, and determines what policy areas are discussed by the voting population. Media focus on certain topics can influence the subsequent actions taken by representatives in government. In 1965, for example, the media's coverage of the treatment of African American protesters marching from Selma, Alabama to Montgomery, Alabama led to a public outcry that resulted in the passage of the Voting Rights Act of 1965. The attention the media gives to one policy area over another will significantly affect how important most people think those policy areas are (Whitman-Cobb, 2020).

2.9 CASE STUDY: THE ORIGINS OF U.S. HEALTHCARE POLICY

The desire for some form of national healthcare in the U.S. began in the second half of the nineteenth century. Soon after the U.S. Civil War, the development of germ theory catalyzed the idea that the majority of people could be effectively cured of many different diseases for the first time in human history. Technological advances in preventive care introduced efficient vaccines that would eventually eradicate a number of millennia-old diseases from the planet. While the brilliant scientific discoveries of nineteenth century researchers like Louis Pasteur and Joseph Lister introduced the prospect of living longer lives, they also introduced a new concept unfamiliar to Western civilization at the time: significant medical expense. With the overwhelming benefit of advanced medical technology extending and improving human life came the cost of having to pay for such effective modern practices.

The evolution of healthcare policy in the U.S. has differed significantly from other developed nation-states. American political culture's deep faith in free market capitalism and limited government regulation has been the principle feature driving American healthcare policy decision making for almost 200 years. A historic lack of faith in central government efficiency also hampered the development of government-provided healthcare in the U.S. long after all other economically developed nation-states implemented some form of government-sponsored healthcare.

After World War II, President Harry Truman (1945-1953) became the first American president to whole-heartedly support a national healthcare program. Truman's vision of national healthcare policy reform called for universal comprehensive health insurance for all Americans. In the end, however, the growing Cold War with the Soviet Union and increased fears over socialism swelled the political strength of opponents of government-supported healthcare policy. The defeat of Truman's universal healthcare policies created an environment where private health insurance would be available to Americans who could afford it and publicly funded welfare services would be available to those who could not. After this defeat, advocates of government-supported universal healthcare reform lowered their political expectations to provide basic healthcare insurance for retired, disabled, and indigent Americans. They would finally achieve success with the Johnson administration in the 1960s (Palmer, 1999).

NHE as a % of GDP	
Year	% of GDP
1960	5.0
1970	6.9
1980	8.9
1990	12.1
2000	13.3
2010	17.4

Table 2.4: National Health Expenditures as a Percentage of GDP 1960 – 2010
Source: U.S. Centers for Medicare & Medicaid Services
Attribution: U.S. Centers for Medicare & Medicaid Services
License: Public Domain

President Lyndon Johnson (1963-1969) made another attempt at implementing healthcare reform. Johnson successfully expanded the Social Security Act of 1935 to include healthcare coverage for seniors and the disabled (Medicare) and the poor (Medicaid). The Social Security Act of 1965 made the federal government the largest single purchaser of healthcare services in the country (Moseley, 2008).

Throughout the 1980s and 1990s, healthcare spending dramatically increased in America. President Ronald Reagan's (1981-1989) administration oversaw less government regulation in the healthcare industry and an expansion of private health insurance programs. Reagan's most important healthcare legislation, the Consolidated Omnibus Budget Reconciliation Act of 1986 (COBRA), allowed former employees to remain covered by their previous employer's healthcare program, provided they agreed to pay the full monthly insurance premium (Ross and Hayes 1986).

President Bill Clinton (1993-2001) attempted to restrain the growth of healthcare costs with the Health Security Act of 1993. Clinton's healthcare policy relied on a combination of government provided universal coverage and private insurance providers. Opposition to Clinton's legislation proved too strong and the policy reforms did not survive Congress. Clinton was able to successfully sign the Health Insurance Portability and Accountability Act of 1996 (HIPAA), which increased privacy protections for individuals and required medical providers to make available individual's health records upon request. Clinton also signed legislation creating the Children's Health Insurance Program (CHIP), which expanded Medicaid coverage for uninsured children in families that could not otherwise qualify for Medicaid (Griffin, 2017).

The most significant healthcare reform in recent U.S. history came through the Obama administration (2009-2017). In 2010, President Obama took advantage of Democratic majorities in the U.S. House of Representatives and Senate by signing the Patient Protection and Affordable Care Act (ACA). President Obama's signature legislation prohibited the denial of healthcare insurance to individuals with pre-existing medical conditions, ended the policy of private insurers limiting lifetime coverage for customers, extended the coverage of Americans on their parent's health insurance to the age of twenty-six, provided basic requirements that all insurance plans must include, and required all Americans to acquire health insurance (individual mandate). In addition, the ACA expanded Medicaid coverage for those eligible (and in states that participated) while providing federal subsidies to lower and middle-income Americans to assist in the purchase of private health insurance. In general, the ACA was designed to build on the U.S. foundation of employer-backed healthcare coverage (60% of Americans receive healthcare through employers) and fill in the coverage gaps by expanding Medicaid and providing tax credits to make coverage more affordable for the lower income middle-class population (Garfield et al., 2019). While the Obama administration successfully passed healthcare reform policy, the actors involved traveled a difficult political road to get there.

As we mentioned earlier, the 2008 elections resulted in Democratic majorities in the U.S. House of Representatives (257-199) and Senate (59-41). The Democrat's fifty-nine seats in the Senate—which included two independents who caucused with the Democratic party—were particularly important because they left the party one seat shy of a filibuster-proof supermajority. In April of 2009, Senator Arlen Spector, a Republican from Pennsylvania, changed political parties and joined the Democrats. With a strong majority in the House and a filibuster-proof majority in the Senate, President Obama's healthcare reform legislation achieved a realistic chance of becoming the law of the land (Garfield et al., 2019).

The Democrat's complete control of the Senate did not last long. In August of 2009, Senator Ted Kennedy of Massachusetts died, leaving his party with fifty-nine seats in the Senate. A January 2010 special election would allow the people of Massachusetts to select a permanent replacement. With their complete control of a united government intact, the Democratic party successfully passed the ACA in the House of Representatives on November 7, 2009 (220-215) and in the Senate on December 24, 2009 (60-39) (Price and Norbeck, 2014).

While passing landmark healthcare reform legislation in the House and Senate was an important milestone, it was far from the end of the legislative process. Legislation that has been successfully voted out of the House and Senate must be sent to a conference committee in order to reconcile the many differences that exist between the two versions of the bill. Conference committees comprise members of both chambers of Congress who must agree on significant changes to the Senate and House versions of any legislation, often a monumentally difficult task to perform. The product of conference committee negotiations must then be sent back to both chambers for a final vote on the legislation before it is sent to the president for signature or veto. Given the Democratic party's control of the House and Senate on Christmas Day, 2009, few expected they would have any difficulty getting the ACA through this last hurdle and on to the president's desk. Those expectations turned out to be wrong.

The special election on January 19, 2010, in which the people of Massachusetts would select a permanent replacement for the late Senator Kennedy, provided an overwhelmingly surprising outcome. Republican Scott Brown, who ran on an anti-ACA platform, pulled off one of the more unexpected political victories in U.S. Senate history by winning the special election and becoming the first Republican Senator from the Commonwealth of Massachusetts since 1972. This upset victory by the Republicans deprived the Democratic party of their filibuster-proof sixtieth seat in the Senate prior to conference committee action.

President Obama and Speaker of the House Nancy Pelosi thus faced a unique political dilemma. Although the ACA had successfully passed through both chambers of the federal legislative branch, the Senate and House versions of the bill had to be identical before the president could sign it into law. The traditional method of this process would require a successful vote from both chambers on a conference committee's version of the two bills. Without their sixtieth seat in the Senate, Democrats would be unable to prevent a Republican filibuster from "killing" the legislation at the literal last minute. To overcome this problem, Democratic leadership used an unconventional approach that would not require conference committee action. Democrats sent the House of Representatives the exact copy of the Senate bill for a vote. If the House approved the Senate version of the ACA in its entirety, there would be no need for conference committee action or a future Senate vote that would certainly be filibustered by Republicans. On March 21, 2010, House Democrats successfully passed the Senate version of the bill (219-212). President Obama signed the Patient Protection and Affordable Care Act on March 23, 2010 (Price and Norbeck, 2014).

Successful navigation through the legislative and executive branches of the federal government was not the end of the political story for the ACA. As discussed above, the judicial branch represents another important actor in the public policy process. State governments, interest groups, and individual citizens (also important actors in the policy process) immediately challenged the constitutionality of the ACA after it became federal law.

Twenty-six state governments and the National Federation of Independent Business challenged two specific provisions within the ACA on constitutional grounds: the individual mandate requiring individuals to purchase healthcare insurance or pay a penalty and the required expansion of Medicaid coverage by state governments to include all individuals at or below 138% of the poverty level. Opponents of the ACA argued that the individual mandate was outside the constitutional power of Congress to regulate commerce or lay and collect taxes. The required expansion of Medicaid was argued to be a violation of the Tenth Amendment and a violation of the state governments' right to exercise all reserved powers not specifically denied to the states by the Constitution. The Supreme Court's 2012 opinion in *National Federation of Independent Business v. Sebelius* upheld Congressional power to create the individual mandate (as a legitimate power to tax enumerated in Article One of the Constitution) and allowed the Medicaid expansion program to continue if state governments volunteered to participate.

President Donald Trump's (2017-2019) healthcare platform included repealing and replacing the ACA. The Trump administration pushed for adoption of the American Health Care Act in 2017. Despite Republican majorities in the U.S. House of Representatives and Senate, President Trump was unsuccessful in replacing the ACA. Although the ACA remains the law of the land, the Trump administration limited its effectiveness by reducing federal funding for outreach and enrollment assistance programs and removing the individual mandate requirement (Garfield et al., 2019).

2.10 CRITICAL THINKING QUESTIONS – ORIGINS AND ACTORS IN POLICY MAKING AND THE ACA

- How did nineteenth century breakthroughs in medical technology affect healthcare policy making in the U.S.?

- What factors made the evolution of healthcare policy in the U.S. different than other developed nation-states?

- What were the signature elements of the Obama administration's Patient Protection and Affordable Care Act?

- How was the judicial branch an actor in the policy making process regarding the ACA? How were interest group actors in the policy making process? How were state governments involved involved in the policy making process?

2.11 CHAPTER SUMMARY

The American Revolution against the British Empire gave rise to contemporary policy making in the U.S. The Constitution created a new system of government (federalism) that has continuously evolved from its birth in 1787. Initially, the new federal government was responsible for few policy areas outside of foreign affairs and public infrastructure. However, as the growing nation-state's demands for more services and regulations from the federal government began to increase, the federal government expanded into policy areas that had previously been the exclusive domain of state governments.

Policy making at the national level involves a number of different actors. Constitutional actors, comprising the three branches of the federal government, were specifically created by the U.S. Constitution. These constitutional actors (legislative, executive, and judicial branches) possess policy making powers that are purposefully intertwined with the other constitutional actors. While attempting to prevent the rise of tyrannical forces in any one branch of government, these checks-and-balances, created by the separation of powers doctrine, make policy making difficult. Non-constitutional actors are influential in the policy making process as well. Non-elected bureaucrats, citizens, interest groups, and the media impact the policy making decisions of the constitutional actors on a variety of different issues.

2.12 KEY TERMS

- Concurrent powers
- Confederate government
- Enumerated powers
- Executive orders
- Federalism
- Great Society
- Implied powers
- Judicial activism
- Judicial restraint
- Judicial review
- New Deal
- Power
- Reserved powers
- Unitary government

2.13 REFERENCES

Bardes, Barbara, and Robert Oldendick. 2012. *Public Opinion Measuring the American Mind*. New York. Rowan & Littlefield.

Baum, Lawrence. 2019. *The Supreme Court*. Washington D.C. CQ Press.

Bond, Jon, and Kevin Smith. 2016. *Analyzing American Democracy*. New York. Routledge Taylor & Francis Group.

Calvi, James, and Susan Coleman. 2004. *American Law and Legal Systems*. Upper Saddle River. Pearson Publishing.

Dahl, Robert. 1961. *Who Governs? Democracy and Power in an American City*. New Haven. Yale University Press.

Garfield, Rachel, Kendal Orgera, and Anthony Damico. 2019. *The Uninsured and the ACA: A Primer*. Kaiser Family Foundation.

Ginsberg, Benjamin, Theodore Lowi, Margaret Weir, Caroline Tolbert, Andrea Campbell, and Robert Spitzer. 2019. *We the People An Introduction to American Politics*. New York. W.W. Norton & Company.

Goodsell, Charles. 1983. *The Case For Bureaucracy*. Chatham. Chatham House Publishers.

Greenstein, Fred. 1995. *Leadership in the Modern Presidency*. Boston. Harvard University Press.

Griffin, Jeff. 2017. *The History of Healthcare in America*. JP Griffin Group. www.griffinbenefits.com/employeebenefitsblog/history-of-healthcare.com

Johannes, John. 2016. *Thinking About Political Reform How to Fix, or Not Fix, American Government and Politics*. New York. Oxford University Press.

Kernell, Samual, and Gary Jacobson, Thad Kousser, and Lynn Vavreck. 2018. *The Logic of American Politics*. Washington D.C. CQ Press.

Kollman, Ken. 2015. *The American Political System*. New York. W.W. Norton & Company.

Mann, Thomas, and Norman Ornstein. 2006. *The Broken Branch How Congress Is Failing America and How to Get it Back on Track*. New York. Oxford University Press.

McClain, Paula, and Steven Tauber. 2016. *American Government in Black and White*. New York: Oxford University Press.

Milkis, Sidney, Michael Nelson. 2016. *The American President Origins and Development*. Washington D.C. CQ Press.

Moseley, George. 2008. *The U.S. Health Care Non-System 1908-2008*. AMA Journal of Ethics. journalofethics.ama-assn.org/article/us-health-care-non-system-1908-2008/2008-05

O'Brien, David. 2017. *Constitutional Law and Politics Struggles for Power and Governmental Accountability*. New York. W.W. Norton & Company.

Palmer, Karen. 1999. *A Brief History: Universal Health Care Efforts in the U.S.* Transcribed from a talk given at the Physicians for a National Health Program Meeting. San Francisco CA.

Price, Gary, and Tim Norbeck. 2014. *A Look Back at How the President Was Able to Sign Obamacare Into Law Four Years Ago*. Forbes Physicians Foundation.

Roskin, Michael, Robert Cord, James Medeiros, and Walter Jones. 2017. *Political Science An Introduction*. New York. Pearson Publishing.

Ross, Mary, and Carol Hayes. 1986. *Consolidated Omnibus Budget Reconciliation Act of 1985*. Social Security Bulletin. Vol. 49. 8.

Simon, Douglas, Joseph Romance, and Neal Riemer. 2020. *The Challenge of Politics*. Washington D.C. CQ Press.

Stith, Kate. 1988. "Congress' Power of the Purse." *Yale Law Journal*. Vol 97. 7.

Van Geel, T.R. 2005. *Understanding Supreme court Opinions*. New York. Pearson Publishing.

Vile, John. 2010. *A Companion to the United States Constitution and its Amendments*. New York. Rowman & Littlefield Publishers.

Vile, John. 2010. *Essential Supreme Court Decisions Summaries of Leading Cases in U.S. Constitutional Law*. New York. Rowman & Littlefield Publishers.

Wasserman, Gary. 2015. *The Basics of American Politics*. Boston. Pearson Publishing.

Weber, Max.1968 org. 1922. *Economy and Society: An Outline of Interpretive Sociology*. New York: Bedminster Press.

Whitman-Cobb, Wendy. 2020. *Political Science Today*. Washington D.C. CQ Press.

3 Foundations of the Policy Process

3.1 CHAPTER OBJECTIVES:

- Discuss the differences between public policy and politics.
- Explore the factors that lead the government to create policy.
- Evaluate the various theories of public policy making.
- Summarize the stages of the policy process.

The Great Depression and WWII eras in American history marked a period of rapidly increasing federal government intervention into public policy that had, at one time, been under the purview of state and local governments. For instance, during the 20th century, the federal government passed far reaching policies meant to expand civil rights, decrease poverty, protect the environment, and safeguard workers. After years of expansion, the Reagan presidency ushered in a period of government reductions. President Reagan stated in his first inaugural address: "Government is not the solution to our problems; government is the problem." He and many others felt that the government should not interfere with the invisible hand of the market; in other words, "no policy is good policy." This philosophy lead to a decline in the role of government and a desire for policies and services, once provided by the government, to be supported by the private sector and markets. Since that time, many government services have been outsourced to private companies, including defense contractors, private prisons, and private school bus drivers, just to name a few.

The evolution of policy in America, and the ongoing debate surrounding government versus private sector obligations, deserves greater attention. When should the government act, and when should the private sector address public problems? In the following sections, we will address the role and limitations of the government in policy making and assess the goals of public policy. This chapter will also discuss the stages model of the policy process, after which, we will evaluate the ability of the stages model to help us better understand how public policy is made.

3.2 WHEN SHOULD GOVERNMENT ACT?

Governments wield the power to influence the actions of individuals, groups, and private sector organizations, as well as the power to punish those who do not follow the established laws of the land. While this may appear to be an overwhelmingly oppressive view of government, it is not necessarily as alarming as it may first appear. Governments in liberal democracies (like the U.S.) primarily exist to serve the public by providing services that cannot or would not be provided by the **market**. The market describes a social system in which individuals pursue their own self-interest by exchanging goods and services with others in a way that is mutually beneficial (Stone, 2002). We will explore the relationship between the market and public policy in the following sections.

3.3 MARKET FAILURES

Market failures occur when there is an inefficient allocation of goods and services by the free market. Governments often use market failures as a rationale for intervening in economic activity: "Put simply, governments act when markets fail to achieve the conditions that justify their use" (Stewart Hedge & Lester, 2008). According to Weimer and Vining (2017), market failures occur due to one of four reasons: **public goods**, **externalities**, **natural monopolies**, and **information asymmetry**.

Figure 3.1: National defense is a public good.
Source: U.S. Army
Attribution: Thomas Cieslak
License: Public Domain

One of the most important actions governments can take involves the provision or protection of public goods. Public goods refer to the common goods enjoyed by everyone in society (Samuelson, 1955). Public goods cannot be limited to only those individuals who choose to pay for them because they are naturally available to all. Clean air, streetlights, and public roads are examples of public goods. National defense exemplifies a pure public good. One person can benefit from national defense without reducing the benefit another person receives. Similarly, one cannot be excluded from the benefits national defense provides.

Public goods cannot be provided or ensured by the market (private sector) due to two of their unique characteristics: non-**exclusion** and joint consumption, also referred to as non-**rivalrous** (Samuelson, 1954). Non-exclusion describes the inability to prevent individuals from enjoying a public good. Joint consumption describes the ability of one person to consume a public good without precluding others from enjoying it. This phenomenon is referred to as non-rivalrous, since the market cannot exclude those who do not pay for a public good from enjoying it. Because exclusion is impossible, the market also cannot ensure a profitable return if they were to provide a public good (Schneider and Ingram, 1997).

Government actions protecting public goods occured in the U.S. federal government's passage of the Clean Air Act of 1970 (an amended version of earlier air pollution acts from the 1950s and 1960s). This legislation vastly expanded federal and state government's power to regulate air pollutants from stationary and mobile sources. The federal and state government's subsequent regulation of air pollution in the U.S. has served to dramatically reduce dangerous pollutants in the air. Clean air is a public good that can only be protected by government action. Services that are not generally provided by the market involve those in which profits are impossible to ensure. Since clean air is nonexclusive (you cannot stop individuals from breathing clean air) and involves joint consumption (my breathing clean air does not stop you from breathing it), the private sector has no incentive to make any attempts at providing it. Although some companies have tried, it is difficult to profit by selling clean air.

Government actions to protect clean air, water, public lands, and other natural resources are considered vital due to the inability of other actors in the policy process to protect them. As described in Hardin's article (1968) *The Tragedy of the Commons*, commonly held resources ("common pool resources") must be protected by government actions. If individual and private sector actors were allowed to consume or abuse publicly owned natural resources without government regulations, those natural resources would be depleted and unavailable to future generations. The federal government's passage of the National Environmental Policy Act (NEPA) of 1970 exemplifies government action to protect common pool resources. The act requires all government projects to consider their possible impact on the environment. Environmental impact statements are required before any federal government project, or projects involving federal funding, can take place. Most state governments have subsequently enacted their own versions of NEPA to provide protections for common pool resources that could not be provided by the private sector.

Conversely, a **private good** is both rivalrous and excludable. A pure private good is one that is privately owned and, once consumed, cannot be consumed by another. A coffee from Starbucks is a prime example of such an item. The person who bought the coffee is not required to share and, once they consume the coffee, it cannot be consumed again. Some private goods are not pure private goods; instead, they are considered toll goods. Toll roads, for example, exclude motorists who are unable or unwilling to pay the toll. However, one motorist's consumption, or use, of the road does not prevent another motorist from using the same road. Similarly, some public goods are not pure public goods. These goods are not excludable but are rivalrous. Public fisheries, including rivers, lakes, and streams, are open to the public, but consumption of the fish is limited if catching and eating too many fish would deplete the population, the act of catching and releasing a fish would not apply to this scenario.

	Rivalrous	Non-Rivalrous
Excludable	Pure Private Goods:	Toll Goods:
	Food, Clothing, Computers	Toll Roads, Cable TV
Non-Excludable	Common Property:	Pure Public Goods:
	Fisheries	National Defense

Table 3.1: Public vs. Private Goods.
Source: Original Work
Attribution: Keith Lee
License: CC BY-SA 4.0

Externalities (Stigler, 1961) refer to effects resulting from a produced good that are not the intent of production. One example is the effect on a local economy when a major sporting event takes place, such as the Super Bowl, the NBA playoffs, or the Master's golf tournament. Businesses not directly related to or responsible for the event will still benefit from the occasion due to visitors frequenting their establishments. This type of spillover effect is considered a positive externality since the effect benefits the community. Conversely, a negative externality includes water and air pollution created by coal-fired power plants. The power plants provide a service to the community, but the service comes at a price beyond the monthly power bill. Air quality and water quality are reduced, and profit-maximizing firms do not have an incentive to expend resources to limit their environmental impact. Government intervention is required to address this failure by setting restrictions on how much pollution can be generated and fining firms for exceeding established limits.

Natural monopolies (Baumol, 1970) can occur when start-up costs are high, thereby making it impractical for multiple firms to provide a service. Examples include public utilities, such as water, sewer, and gas services. Utilities require infrastructure to provide the resource, which is a costly endeavor. Furthermore, having multiple water, gas, or sewer lines is not practical considering the complexity of pipeline networks. The government generally intervenes to provide the utility or, at a minimum, negotiates prices to ensure citizens are not excluded by being priced out of the resource.

Lastly, **information asymmetry** (Akerlof, 1970) occurs when a firm possesses knowledge that the consumer does not. For example, prescription drug providers know about adverse side effects due to drug testing and would benefit from not disclosing this information. However, the Federal Drug Administration (FDA) requires prescription drug companies to provide sufficient information to protect the consumer. Consider the work that government agencies do to protect the public and ensure that consumers have the information they need to make choices about food products. Non-GMO food labels, grading meat packages, warning labels on cigarettes and alcoholic beverages: the government requires companies to place these labels on products because, otherwise, the food packaging industry is unlikely to disclose negative information to consumers. These are all examples of market failures that resulted in government intervention.

3.4 LARGE-SCALE RESOURCE COORDINATION

Government action is required in the provision of resources that would not otherwise be available to the general population. The construction of the U.S. interstate highway system would have been unimaginable without the vast economic resources available to federal and state governments. Federal and state funding for public universities enables a larger percentage of the general public to have access to secondary education. Publicly funded hospitals allow state and local governments to increase the public's access to healthcare, especially in rural areas. Publicly funded sewage systems, water treatment facilities, water drainage infrastructure, and public health regulations are all examples of government actions that, in general, are not efficiently provided by private actors (McClain and Tauber, 2016).

A number of examples exist of times when the vast resources of national and state governments make them the only actors in the policy process that have the ability to act in the public's interest. Natural disasters like hurricanes, earthquakes, tornadoes, wildfires, and tsunamis are responsible for unimaginable levels of destruction to public and private property that often cost billions of dollars to repair. More important than the financial costs associated with natural disasters is the expedited effort required to rescue the survivors of such incidents. Often, national/state/local governments are the only actors with the resources available to coordinate large scale disaster relief efforts.

3.5 GOVERNMENT FAILURES

Government failures occur when a government does not leave society better off, particularly in the context of correcting market failures. Gupta (2011; see also Weimer and Vining, 2017) provides ten reasons for government failure:

1. Inability to Define Social Welfare
2. Limits of Democracy and the Paradox of Voting
3. Inability to Define the Marginal Costs and Benefits of Public Goods
4. Political Constraints
5. Cultural Constraints
6. Institutional Constraints
7. Legal Constraints
8. Knowledge Constraints
9. Analytical Constraints
10. Timing of Policies

Government failure that stems from an inability to define social welfare typically occurs due to the ambiguity of the term "social welfare." As we will discuss later, ambiguous terms are hard to analyze due to their multiple, and often personal, meanings. As such, there is no sufficient way to intervene in market failures that center around needs that cannot be clearly articulated.

Second, democracy hinders government intervention because of the unpredictable nature of voters and those who have agenda-setting power. The *paradox of voting* brings into question the common assumption that voting outcomes reflect the "will of the people" (Weimer & Vining, 2017). Instead, if a voter's first choice candidate has little chance of getting a majority of the votes, as is the case with 3rd party candidates, the voter may find it advantageous to vote for a less preferred but more viable candidate instead of "wasting" their vote on a candidate with little chance of winning. This scenario results in the election of a candidate who many not reflect the true policy preferences of the people.

A third reason government intervention is limited comes from the inability to adequately calculate marginal costs and benefits due to the nature of public goods. For example, public roads and highways certainly provide benefits, but how can their costs be adequately measured? The costs associated with hiring contractors can be accounted for, but the impact on drivers having to detour during construction or any environmental effects are less clear. Similarly, benefits cannot be sufficiently measured. The new road may reduce congestion and traffic accidents which could lead to improved motorist well-being, but well-being is not quantifiable.

The next set of reasons listed by Gupta are a series of constraints: political, cultural, institutional, legal, knowledge-based, and analytical. Political constraints refer to the inability to enact new policy due to the unwillingness of politicians. Policies can be proposed that may be effective at correcting a market failure, but without enough support from political actors, the proposal becomes a moot point. Similarly, cultural constraints exist when members of the affected community do not buy in to the proposed policy. Elected officials may not be willing to risk political capital to pass a policy if it could affect their reelection prospects. Therefore, regardless of their certainty in the proposal's ability at correcting the market, they may deem it as not in their best interest to support that policy.

Institutional and legal constraints refer to the structure of those implementing policy (see chapter 6). These restraints refer to the policy maker and implementers working within a specific legal framework. For example, the gun control debate is a major policy issue in the U.S., and the argument for or against gun control largely depends on how one interprets the Second Amendment. The Constitution is the legal framework which policy makers must consider before enacting, or refusing to enact, gun control. Knowledge constraints arise when the evidence related to a policy proposal is speculative at best. For example, a state deciding to legalize marijuana before another state must rely on projection models to determine if the costs outweigh the benefits, which, as discussed above, is hard to adequately define. However, once one state implements the policy, it opens the door for other states to follow the example it provides. Policymakers will have more evidence on policy success as more states enact the policy. The last constraint, analytical constraints, occur when policy justification relies heavily on quantitative analysis. The analytics are generally computed in the proposal or implementation stage and would need to be replicated in the analysis stage to determine if the original analysis was conducted objectively, for example, determining that the policymaker did not shape the results to increase favor for the proposed policy.

Lastly, the final reason provided by Gupta is the timing of policies. According to Gupta, four issues relating to the timing of policies constrain policymakers: recognition gap, prescription lag, adoption lag, and implementation lag. Policymakers must look at trends and predict changes well before they occur to prevent the policy from being enacted too late. However, it is nearly impossible to predict issues that arise which might affect the social welfare of society; therefore, the issue may not be recognized in time to address the problem. Prescription, adoption, and implementation lags refer to the time constraints from issue recognition to program implementation. Each stage, including proposal, adoption, and implementation, moves slowly, thus further hindering policymakers from correcting failures even if the problem is recognized early.

3.6 WHAT VALUES SHOULD GOVERNMENTS PURSUE?

One of the most common justifications for government intervention stems from the public's desire to promote the values with which citizens generally agree. The normative values pursued by governments in contemporary liberal democracies can generally be found outlined in written constitutions. For example, the U.S.

Constitution's preamble requires the federal government to preserve a number of national values like the establishment of justice, ensuring domestic tranquility, providing for the common defense, and promoting the general welfare. In democracies, like the U.S., the values of individual economic liberty and representative government are of paramount importance (Parsons, 2020).

American sociologist Robin Williams (1970) wrote about the basic values that American citizens embrace. He argued that many of the values and ideals shared by Americans are rooted in the country's history. These values are freedom, individualism, pragmatism, volunteerism, mobility, patriotism, progress, and the American Dream. The idea of freedom shaped the framer's beliefs about the role of government. Many of the freedoms enjoyed today are enshrined in the Bill of Rights, including freedom of speech, assembly, press, etc. Governments often express the value of freedom when policy makers make decisions governing liberties that can be legitimately denied by government. We may not think of governments denying freedoms to some as a vehicle for protecting the freedom of others, but it is a policy tool that is used quite often. For example, the government limits your liberty to speak (slander) or write (libel) harmful lies about others. Your freedom to enjoy a few glasses of wine while driving down the interstate is denied by a government that values the freedom of others to drive on safe roads. More recently, several state governments determined that the freedom of citizens at risk of becoming ill from the COVID-19 pandemic superseded the freedom of those citizens who refused to wear a face mask.

America's sense of individualism has been a consistent theme throughout history, from Thomas Jefferson who argued that individual identity should be sacred and is tied to dignity and integrity, to pioneers who explored the west and those farmers and business owners driven by self-sufficiency. Individualism refers to not only self-reliance but also an American ideal of economic self-sufficiency and the strongly held belief that individuals must strive to "pull themselves up by their bootstraps." We continue to see remnants of a strong sense of individualism when controversial policies are discussed, for instance, with arguments against redistributive policies such as welfare, Medicaid,

Figure 3.2: Facemasks during the Covid-19 pandemic became a point of contention between some Americans and state and local governments.
Source: Flickr
Attribution: Paul Becker
License: CC BY 2.0

and universal health care. Individualism ties into pragmatism, as Americans are known for their "can-do" spirit and focus on invention to solve problems. Likewise, the American desire to volunteer reflects an optimistic belief that citizens can solve problems rather than wait for others to step in.

Mobility refers to the American willingness to solve problems or increase economic mobility by moving elsewhere to make a fresh start. Americans are constantly seeking a way to better themselves, either through business, education, or simply changing their environment. The concept of mobility is related to the American value of progress as it pertains to the desire to make use of opportunities. For instance, immigrants often argue that they moved to the U.S. to build wealth and improve the lives of their children. This value is motivated by an American standard of hard work and sacrifice for the sake of generations to come. The "American Dream" stems from these values and continues to influence policy even today.

Patriotism plays a prominent role in the values that Americans share. As Williams writes, "National pride has become generally stronger than regional pride. The prevalence of patriotic symbols: flags fly in suburban neighborhoods, bumper stickers announce 'I'm proud to be American,' the national anthem is played at every sporting event. National holidays such as Thanksgiving and Independence Day intensify the sense of national identity" (Williams, 1970).

Finally, **equality** is a value pursued by governments when laws are passed that mandate the equal treatment of individuals within society (Stone, 2002). The U.S. government's passage of the Civil Rights Act of 1964, for example, was meant to improve political and social equality for minority groups and women in the U.S. The U.S. Supreme Court recently interpreted the Civil Rights Act's prohibition of discrimination based on sex to include protections for same-sex couples (*Bostock v. Clayton County GA*, 2020) and transgender communities (*Harris Funeral Homes v. EEOC*, 2020).

> ### Stop and Think
>
> What values should governments pursue? How have values changed in the U.S. over time? Are the same values that were important in 1970 important today?

The U.S. Supreme Court has been instrumental in advancing equality in areas involving public education (*Brown v. Board of Education*, 1954), interracial marriage (*Loving v. Virginia*, 1967), and same-sex marriage (*Obergefell v. Hodges*, 2015).

It is important to note that simply because a nation upholds a set of core values does not mean that those values will be guaranteed for all. Many examples exist over the course of U.S. history when freedoms have been denied to individuals and groups. Furthermore, values become more or less of a focus in American society based on direct pressure and tension between changing demographics, politics, and political culture. For instance, the 1980s brought about a resurgence of the conservative focus on family values. After 9/11, individual freedoms were less of a concern due to national security issues and the threat of terrorism. Most recently, the U.S. has witnessed an increased focus on patriotism and a renewed sense of individualism (McCourtney Institute, Penn State, 2019). Changing values are expected and often serve as catalysts for policy change and innovation.

3.7 WHAT IS THE GOAL OF PUBLIC POLICY?

Governments have the authority to act on a wide variety of issues, although they do not act on every public issue as we will learn in chapter 4. Often, the decision to act is a result of public consensus that collective action is desired and/or necessary (Stewart, Hedge, Lester, 2008). John Locke (1689) famously described the time before governments were established as the *state of nature*. In the state of nature life, liberty, and property are continuously threatened because there are no laws for protection. Once citizens decide they would rather live in an ordered and stable society, they agree to a social contract or an agreement among the members of that society to cooperate and form a government that must then pass policies safeguarding individual rights. Once citizens are secure, they are then free to pursue opportunities and contribute to the betterment of society. This idea is the ultimate goal of public policy in a **liberal democracy**: ensure that citizens are free to fulfill their aspirations.

Mintrom (2012) discusses the actions that governments must take to ensure that citizens are able to pursue their goals and contribute to society. Mintrom's list is by no means comprehensive; nevertheless, it does provide context for understanding the central goals that public policy attempts to achieve.

First, governments must create policies that defend people and property while maintaining public order. Societies unaccustomed to war and lawlessness often take for granted the importance of survival and a general sense of wellbeing. If, for instance, citizens are constantly under threat of violence, or living in a war zone, the ability to safely raise a family and/or to work are severely threatened. For this reason, policies must be created with the goal of defending people and property. This includes both military threats abroad and domestic threats of crime or violence. Establishing military power and maintaining a corruption free police force strengthens security and helps keep the peace "so that citizens can confidently engage in social and economic activities that can enrich their lives and the lives of others, without being threatened by other people or adverse natural events" (Mintrom, 2019).

Policies should support effective nongovernmental institutions. This concept is similar to preventing market failures, as people often look to government when they want institutional change. In fact, "many public policies are government efforts to reform and improve the workings of the broader set of societal institutions" (Mintrom, 2019). Consider regulatory policy, which is meant to curtail the negative costs of business activities. Environmental regulations that reduce carbon emissions or restrict the types of chemicals that can be used in household cleaners, and laws that prohibit monopolies are all examples of policies that encourage effective nongovernmental institutions. Greater efficiency can also be achieved through these types of policies. For instance, governments can promote efficient economic advancement which in turn leads to human advancement. Promotion of small businesses or lowering interest rates during a recession are examples of efficient economic policies.

Recent attention on sustainability has encouraged government intervention in sustainable development. Most would agree that our world is fueled by a collection of finite resources. However, the desire and ability of individual governments to put sustainable policies into action varies from country to country. Governments that choose to promote sustainability do so through regulations, taxes and incentives, fees and subsidies. For example, tax benefits are given to homeowners who use energy efficient products, such as solar panels or electric cars.

Finally, Mintrom argues that the goal of policy is to promote human flourishing and prosperity. Policies that promote human flourishing can address individuals or communities. Community planning efforts, economic and educational opportunities, and social welfare systems are all government attempts to enhance the human experience and allow citizens to advance and improve. Likewise, policies that promote social equity benefit citizens because they confirm a commitment and respect for human dignity. As Mintrom writes, "As a society, we gain immeasurably from the fully developed actions, creativity, discoveries, and tenacity of other human beings" (Mintrom, 2019). Policies that promote social equity also serve another benefit by promoting social order. Recent racial inequalities have highlighted how views that government institutions, such as Congress or police officers who behave unfairly, can damage public trust and increase levels of social unrest. Along these same lines, advancement of human rights and promotion of civil rights are actions that governments can take to promote human flourishing.

3.8 CONCEPTUALIZING THE POLICY PROCESS

So far in this chapter we have discussed what circumstances lead to government action, what values governments should pursue, and the goals that guide policy making. Next, we make sense of policy by articulating the steps that proposed policies take through the political process, beginning with problem identification and ending with a comprehensive evaluation. These steps are not all encompassing; the policy process is messy and rarely moves smoothly from one phase to the next, but students of policy may find that the basic stages model provides a helpful guide to understanding an imperfect process.

3.9 STAGES HEURISTIC MODEL OF PUBLIC POLICYMAKING

The stages heuristic model of public policymaking is by far the most studied and utilized theory explaining the policy process. Public policymaking in the U.S. occurs in numerous stages and includes an assortment of policy actors, such as elected politicians, bureaucrats, interest groups, and even citizens. Harold Laswell (1951, 1956) was one of the first scholars to elaborate on a multi-stage decision process of public policy making. The stages that he described have evolved but generally include the following steps: (1) problem identification, (2) agenda setting, (3) policy formulation, (4) policy legitimation, (5) policy implementation, and (6) evaluation (Figure 3.1). The following summaries are meant to give students context and an overview of the policy stages. Each concept is discussed in greater detail in later chapters: problem identification and agenda setting (chapter 4), policy formulation (chapter 5), implementation (chapter 6), and evaluation (chapter 7).

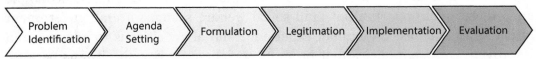

Figure 3.3: The Policymaking Process
Source: Original Work
Attribution: Kimberly Martin
License: CC BY-SA 4.0

3.9.1 Step One: Problem Identification

The first step in the policy making process is to identify a public problem. Problem identification is more difficult than it may seem; while one person or group may believe there is a problem, another group may not. Similarly, one group may define the problem differently than another. These complexities cause problem identification to be inherently political. Consider the recent debate about removing confederate statues. Many states have policies that prohibit their removal without permission from the state legislature. Interested groups, such as supporters of the Black Lives Matter movement, have argued that the monuments are a symbol of inequality. Others feel that they are a symbol of heritage and Southern pride. Both groups fundamentally disagree that there is even a public problem. The likelihood that they will ever agree on the same solution is low. As this example illustrates, the process of identifying and defining public problems is complex.

3.9.2 Step Two: Agenda Setting

Once a problem has been identified, the next step in the policy making process is to attract the attention of policymakers, thus encouraging them to include the problem on their personal agenda. Agendas are lists of public problems that are of importance to individual policymakers. Similarly, the public agenda includes all the issues that may or may not be seriously considered for government intervention. Issues may become less important over time and leave the agenda only to reappear when indicators or focusing events increase their importance. For instance, the national budget deficit was an important topic on the public agenda during the 2012 presidential campaign, while in 2016 resolving the deficit was not as important.

3.9.3 Step Three: Policy Formulation

After a public problem has received attention from policymakers, it must be formulated and articulated into a policy in written form. Policy formulation is a complex process. During this stage, the benefits and drawbacks of each proposal are debated and considered. Policymakers must then decide who will be tasked with carrying out the policy and what that process of implementation will look like. They must also consider how they will encourage citizens to follow the new law. Will they receive a punishment if they neglect to abide by the new rule or a reward if they do?

3.9.4 Step Four: Policy Legitimation

Policy legitimation is the step in the policy making process that students have likely studied. American government classes teach students how a bill becomes a law and this step is no different. You will recall that public policy is made at the local, state, and federal levels of government. Generally, elected members of a congress or general assembly propose policy. They then send their proposals, better known as bills, to a smaller committee that specializes on the topic of the bill so that it can be debated and considered. If the committee sees the bill favorably, they will pass it on to the entire elected body who will then vote on the proposed policy. Bills that pass successfully through each chamber—Senate and House of Representatives—are then sent to the president or governor who signs or vetoes the policy. This process is far more complex than this short explanation might lead you to believe, but the steps are critical for public policy to gain legitimacy and be successfully implemented in the next phase.

3.9.5 Step Five: Policy Implementation

Have you ever wondered what happens to a law after it goes into effect? There is certainly more to the process than simply signing a bill into law and hoping that it is carried out correctly. Policy implementation consists of translating the goals and objectives of a policy into action. During the policy design phase, policymakers either build a roadmap for how policy should be implemented, or they give implementors, who are typically bureaucrats, discretion over how a policy is implemented. For instance, a state passes a resolution that requires law enforcement to increase community policing efforts, essentially promoting stronger community and police relationships. State lawmakers give local police departments the power to determine the best method for increasing community policing, but how should they proceed? Should they require body cameras be worn on duty and punish anyone who chooses not to follow the rule? Should police spend more time in certain neighborhoods or host events in the community? Perhaps they can spend more time in schools with children, or at the very least step up crime prevention measures in violent neighborhoods.

3.9.6 Step Six: Policy Evaluation

The evaluation stage of the policy process provides researchers an opportunity to measure and assess the effectiveness of a particular policy. In chapter 5, we will discuss the intended outcomes of programs and policies in detail. During an evaluation, researchers determine whether the goals of a policy were realized. Did the policy achieve its desired outcome? The result of an evaluation is a recommendation to policymakers regarding whether a program should continue, receive additional funding, or be terminated.

> **Stop and Think**
>
> Of the six steps in the stages model, in which step is a policy more likely to fail? Think of a policy that is currently being debated in politics. Which stage is the policy currently in? In your opinion, is it likely to be successful in this stage?

3.10 ASSESSING THE STAGES MODEL

When Lasswell (1971) began writing about the stages model, he was investigating how policymakers make decisions. Even then, the stages model was meant to describe the policy process rather than create a comprehensive theory of policy making. Charles Jones (1970) argued the same point, that the policy approach is an attempt to "describe a variety of processes designed to complete the policy cycle." Similar to Lasswell, Jones identified what he called the stages of decision making. There have been several iterations of the policy stages from numerous authors over the years (Anderson, 1974, Brewer and deLeon, 1983, Ripley, 1985), but they all broadly encompass the same elements: identification and perception of a public problem, adoption and implementation of the policy, and evaluation or termination of the policy.

The stages model has received its fair share of criticism for producing fragmented research on the policy process. For instance, scholars and students alike often focus research projects on how citizens and even the media have the power to set the agenda. Others focus on the bureaucracy and its skill, or lack of skill, at implementing policy. These separate studies might lead some to believe that the policy process comprises a set of disconnected steps. In some ways this perspective is correct. The policy process does not always proceed perfectly through each stage. Problem identification, for instance, might not occur in an ordered or coherent fashion, and evaluation might not occur at all. Smith and Larimer (2017) argue that creation of a unified model of public policy is a "tall order." The strength of the stages, they argue, is its ability to create a set of manageable frameworks from which we can understand each stage in the process, even if the process is not always precise.

The stages approach may also lead one to believe that the process is linear, meaning that policies progress seamlessly through each step. Once a policy is on the agenda, it is then legitimized, implemented, and finally evaluated. In fact, for some policies, their progression through the process is underscored by a series of "feedback loops." Consider gun control policies that spend most of their time in the problem identification and definition stage. Gun control policies have on occasion progressed to the legitimation phase only to be sent back to agenda setting. A similar account can be made for immigration reform, free college education, and social security reform.

Finally, critics of the stages model argue that it is not particularly scientific, meaning that it is difficult to develop a falsifiable and testable hypothesis. For instance, it is difficult to develop a hypothesis that tests and proves a theory of how problems reach the public agenda. As you will learn in the next chapter, there are many ways for problems to catch the attention of policymakers and advance through the agenda process. This exercise exposes a flaw in the stages model: it is not a theory. The policy stages describe what happens and omit any real explanation for why it happens (Smith and Larimer, 2017). Sabatier (1991) aptly describes the model as the "stages heuristic," meaning that it is a practical method for understanding complex processes. In fact, one of the major advantages of the stages model is that it provides a practical means for understanding and organizing the policy process. Students of public policy often find this approach to be intuitive and logical. As such, the stages heuristic approach is used as a guide for understanding the policy process in this text.

> **Stop and Think**
>
> The stages model is the most commonly used model of policymaking. What are the advantages and disadvantages of the model? What, if anything, is left out of the model and should be included?

3.11 CASE STUDY: HEALTH CARE AS A MARKET FAILURE

Healthcare, or the lack thereof, is a market failure that many argue requires government intervention (Mankiw, 2017). Two indicators of market failure, according to Mankiw, are the prevalence of externalities and market imperfection. Mankiw notes two exemplary externalities: vaccinations and medical research. Vaccines are critical in preventing the spread of disease and the market cannot ensure equal coverage. In an economic sense, preventing disease is a positive externality of healthcare coverage. Similarly, money funneled into healthcare is a positive externality, as it enables research and development which could ultimately lead to medical breakthroughs (e.g., a cure for cancer).

Market imperfections, on the other hand, discourage market intervention, particularly moral hazards and adverse selections. Moral hazards occur when a person engages in a behavior that they would not otherwise participate in if they did not have the protection offered. For example, most people would not jump out of an airplane, but some would if they were offered a parachute. Regarding healthcare coverage, insured individuals may go to the doctor more often than those without insurance because it is available. The coverage (parachute) allows them to visit the doctor for minor needs (jump out of plane) when a lack of coverage would likely induce them to stay home (stay in the plane). Conversely, those without insurance may not seek medical help at all until the problem becomes unbearable. Khullar (2017) reported 20% of uninsured adults admitted going without needed care compared to 3% of insured adults. Waiting to see a doctor delays much needed medical care and results in longer hospital stays, poorer health outcomes, and increased costs for care (Weissman et al., 1991).

Adverse selection, the second market imperfection listed by Mankiw (2017), stems from information asymmetry. The insurer, unaware of which individuals have a chronic illness and which illness it may be, must charge a premium based on unknowns. Naturally, in an effort to protect their bottom line, the insurer is going to charge a higher rate than might be required. This will result in higher premiums, thus pushing healthier people (or people believing they do not need insurance) out of the market. This practice results in a higher proportion of sick people which, in turn, leads to higher premiums, and the process begins again.

Taken together, externalities and market imperfections result in market failure. The government intervened in 2010 with the Affordable Care Act. The law, by providing low or no cost healthcare, should have enhanced positive externalities while minimizing negative externalities. Similarly, the law mandated that everyone have insurance, thus eliminating the problem of adverse selection. However, results were mixed and after lengthy court battles and legislative changes to the way in which the ACA was implemented, many argue that healthcare in the U.S. is still an example of market failure.

3.12 CRITICAL THINKING QUESTION

- Is health care in the U.S. a market failure? Why or why not? Is health care a public problem that can best be solved by the private sector, or is government involvement necessary?

3.13 CHAPTER SUMMARY

This chapter provides a foundation for understanding when and under what circumstances governments choose to act. Governments in liberal democracies primarily exist to serve the public by providing services that cannot or would not be provided by the market. Market failures occur when there is an inefficient allocation of goods and services by the free market. Governments often use market failures as a rationale for intervening in economic activity. However, governments do not always correct market failures. The limits of the democratic process, political, and cultural constraints often result in circumstances where government intervention does not improve society.

The policy making process involves more complexity than simply moving a bill through the legislative process. The stages model allows for greater understanding of the intricacies of the process by highlighting six prominent steps: (1) problem identification, (2) agenda setting, (3) formulation, (4) legitimation, (5) implementation, and (6) evaluation. The policy process does not always proceed perfectly through each stage. The strength of the stages model is its ability to create a set of manageable frameworks from which we can understand each stage in the process, even if the process is not always precise. The stages model provides a foundation to explore the nature of policy making before and after the legislative process even begins. We spend the remainder of this text investigating each step in greater detail.

3.14 KEY TERMS

- Excludable
- Externalities
- Information Asymmetry
- Natural Monopoly
- Public Good
- Private Good
- Rivalrous
- Liberal Democracy
- Liberty
- Market
- Public Goods

3.15 REFERENCES

Akerlof, George A. 1970. "The Market for 'Lemons': Quality Uncertainty and Market. Mechanism." *The Quarterly Journal of Economics*. 84(3): 488-500.

Baumol, William J. 1977. "On the Proper Cost Tests for Natural Monopoly in a Multiproduct Industry." *The American Economic Review*. 67(5): 809-822.

Gupta, Dipak K. 2011. Analyzing Public Policy: Concepts, Tools, and Techniques. Washington, DC: CQ Press.

Hardin, Garrett. 1968. The Tragedy of the Commons. *Science*. Vol. 162, No. 3859.

Khullar, Dhruv. 2017. "As a Doctor, I See How a Lack of Health Insurance Worsens Illness and Suffering." *Washington Post*, January 9, 2017. https://www. washingtonpost.com/news/to-your-health/wp/2017/01/09/doctors-see-how-a-lack-of-health-insurance-exacerbates-illness-and-suffering/

Lasswell, Harold D. 1958. *Politics: Who Gets What, When, How*. New York: Meridian Books.

Mankiw, N. Gregory. 2017. "The Economics of Healthcare."

McClain, Paula, and Steven Tauber. 2016. *American Government in Black and White*. New York, NY. Oxford University Press.

Mintrom, Michael. 2012. *Contemporary Policy Analysis*. New York: Oxford University Press.

Parsons, Craig. 2020. *Introduction to Political Science How to Think for Yourself About Politics*. Boston, MA. Pearson.

Samuelson, Paul A. 1954. "The Pure Theory of Public Expenditure." *The Review of Economics and Statistics*. 36(4): 387-389.

Schneider, Larason, and Helen Ingram. 1997. *Policy Design for Democracy*. Lawrence, KA. University of Kansas Press.

Smith, Kevin, and Larimer, Christopher. 2017. *The Public Policy Theory Primer*. New York: Routledge.

Stigler, George J. 1961. "The Economics of Information." *The Journal of Political Economy*. 69(3): 213-225.

Stone, Deborah. 2002. *Policy Paradox: The Art of Political Decision Making*. New York, NY. W.W. Norton & Company.

"Though Politically Divided, Americans Remain Patriotic." *Penn State University*, 1 July 2019, news.psu.edu/story/578883/2019/07/01/research/though-politically-divided-americans-remain-patriotic.

Weimer, David L and Aidan R. Vining. 2017. Policy Analysis: Concepts and Practice. New York: Routledge.

Weissman JS, Stern R, Fielding SL, Epstein AM. 1991. "Delayed Access To Health Care: Risk Factors, Reasons, And Consequences." *Annals of Internal Medicine*. 114(4): 325-331.

Problem Identification and Agenda Setting

4.1 CHAPTER OBJECTIVES:

- Summarize the processes leading to public policy.
- Evaluate public problems and construct causal stories.
- Explain agenda setting and recognize why it is an important step in the policy process.
- Describe how ideas get on the agenda.
- Explain the various stages of the agenda setting process.
- Identify government actors and their role in the agenda setting process.

In chapter 3, we discussed whether and when governments should act and, if they act, what actions governments should take to solve public problems. In this chapter, we will explore the importance of identifying problems and explain the public agenda in great detail. What is the public agenda, and how does it affect which problems the government addresses? How do policymakers and citizens move problems onto the public agenda?

For most students, learning about the policy making process calls up images of the classic *Schoolhouse Rock* video that tracks a lonely bill from its development to passage through Congress. As with the video, the study of how policy is made generally follows a series of steps or activities meant to simplify the legislative process. What the video does not show is what happens before the bill makes it to committee, before the policymaker has even decided which issues they plan to address. In reality, many of the steps mentioned in the video—committee hearings or the veto process—occur simultaneously or sometimes not at all. The process of identifying public problems receives limited attention, and the video entirely omits the topic of agenda setting. In this chapter, we'll fill in the gaps by studying how politicians, lobbyists, think tanks, and journalists engage in the agenda setting process, all of which results in an imperfect and, at times, complicated system.

4.2 UNDERSTANDING AND IDENTIFYING PROBLEMS

Understanding the origins of public policy requires thorough exploration of the stage of policymaking that American government texts often omit: problem identification. In screenwriter Aaron Sorkin's *The Newsroom,* the character Will McAvoy famously states, "The first step in solving any problem is recognizing there is one." This step in the policy process, that is, in which problems are identified, is critical for policymakers whose responsibility is to design strategies to solve those problems.

What is a policy problem? Policy problems arise from situations or circumstances that cause dissatisfaction for individuals or groups, who then call on the government to find a solution (Anderson, 2015). Governments take action on a vast array of problems, from relief for drought-stricken farmers to nuclear nonproliferation treaties, tax reform, and even safety on school buses. The key to problem identification is what Nelson (1984) describes as *issue recognition.* This stage in the policy process occurs when the problem is first noticed and then perceived to have the potential for government action. Perhaps deep-sea divers notice an excess of plastic items at the bottom of the ocean, or coastal residents experience the oxygen depleting phenomenon known as the red tide. Maybe a college student dies due to hazing, or the number of babies born to drug-addicted mothers increases. These issues, and thousands more, establish a foundation from which future public policy begins.

Issue recognition, therefore, involves identifying and describing the problem and often begins with the questions, "What are the concerns? And what are the causes of my concern?" Let's say that you learn that elementary school students in your neighborhood have lunches withheld when they accumulate a certain amount of unpaid school lunch debt. You are outraged and take the position that lunch should never be withheld from students who, through no fault of their own, are being punished for their parents' misdeeds. In this situation, you have recognized that a problem exists and that it has an identifiable cause: students are not receiving lunch, and the cause is unpaid lunch debt.

The next logical questions are, "Can the situation be improved? And if so, who can improve it?" Certainly, if you are a wealthy individual, you could write a large check to the school district and pay off the debt, if the school accepts that type of donation. You could solicit funds from the community to pay off the debt, but this is a short-term solution since students may accumulate debt again. You could contact the school district and voice your displeasure over the policy or attend a school board meeting. Contacting authority figures is not an uncommon reaction and does, at times, lead to pressure that alleviates a problem. However, you would like to ensure that children never have to worry about missing lunch again, and you believe that government intervention effecting a change in public policy is the only solution to this problem.

Ensuring that a public issue is met with practical solutions requires identifying the level of government that has the responsibility for enacting and implementing specific policies. If you are not sure whether an issue is more suitable for local, state, or federal government intervention, a good rule of thumb is to start at the local level and move to the state or federal arena once other options have been explored. If car break-ins are increasing in your neighborhood, for example, you would not appeal to the U.S. President to solve the local crime problem. If you are having trouble obtaining a fishing permit at a national park, you would not appeal to the Secretary of the Interior. Returning to the school lunch example, each level of government has different levels of authority. School districts have many strategies for dealing with school lunch debt; additionally, what may be possible in one district may not be possible in another. Citizens can always reach out to their local school district and ask to make their meal debt policies public. If the school district's policies result in "food shaming"—students who receive no lunch when debts are unpaid—or other adverse outcomes, then citizens could develop a campaign and hold a rally in the community in an attempt to persuade the school district to change lunch debt policies. If you are satisfied and your campaign is successful, then you may choose not to take the issue to the next government level. Although, circumstances and public outcry could be enough to encourage state or federal action. After the media begins reporting on actual incidences of school "lunch shaming," for example, states could enact legislation to clarify school procedures if students cannot pay for meals.

The likelihood that any given problem will be solved through government action varies. Some policy problems are easy to identify and solve, while others are more complex, difficult to recognize, and have limited solutions. Nevertheless, the problem identification step in the policy process is unavoidable; problems cannot be solved without identifying their underlying cause. Unsurprisingly, identifying the root cause of a problem is often quite tricky. Problem identification is full of controversy, and policymakers often make decisions based on incomplete knowledge of the problem's origins. For example, many communities across the country are grappling with failing schools, low test scores, low attendance rates, and even a shortage of teachers. Decision makers know the problems, but they may be unclear on what exactly causes these problems in the first place. Are failing schools merely a result of poor test-taking skills or ineffective teachers, or do they result from some deeper problem, like low parental involvement, poverty in the school district, or some combination of each?

4.3 ESTABLISHING CAUSALITY

While identifying the root cause of a public problem is complex, the key to finding a policy solution is to establish a link between the problem and its cause. We would not fix a broken arm with a band-aid, yet many of our policy solutions fail to address the underlying cause of public problems and, like band-aids, rely on superficial solutions. Causal stories are a tool that policymakers, interest groups, and even citizens can use to identify more effective solutions. Establishing **causality** allows for the easy creation of models that directly link the effort expended to a particular outcome. The causal stories that result from these models can be employed during policy debates to persuade policymakers to adopt a specific solution.

As an example, policymakers have made several attempts to decrease the rise in obesity and the cost of medical care associated with an unhealthy lifestyle. In 2013, New York City proposed a policy that would limit the size of sugary drinks sold in the city to no more than sixteen ounces (Rinfret, Scheberle, and Pautz, 2019). The goal of the policy was to decrease sugar intake—and, thereby, decrease obesity rates—by limiting the amount of sugar that any one person could purchase and consume. At some point in the problem identification process, policymakers determined that obesity rates were tied to sugar intake. More specifically, they determined that Americans are obese because they consume too much sugar in their beverages.

In the previous example, policymakers created a direct causal link between sugar and obesity, but policy problems are complex and often have many causes. There are numerous ways to explain the rise in obesity rates. Even if you agree with the sugary drink explanation, you could also make the case that lack of exercise, poor overall diet, genetics, and other environmental factors are all responsible for a rise in obesity rates and therefore comprise complexities that would be difficult to address in their entirety. In truth, the government simply does not have enough time or resources to address all public concerns, so policymakers often make tradeoffs between addressing a problem with a partial solution or making the decision not to act at all (Bovaird & Loffler, 2003).

Furthermore, the complexity of establishing causality is regularly overshadowed by politics. Stone (1997) writes that "Causes are objective and can, in principle, be proved by scientific research." Were this truly the case in all circumstances, policy problems might be easier to solve. In reality, "cause and effect are open to interpretation and widely different perceptions" (Stewart, Hedge, Lester, 2008). Often, the individual or group who persuasively demonstrates their own view of causality guides the policy solution or, in some cases, persuades government officials not to act.

Figure 4.1: New York's ban on sugary drinks prompted backlash from the beverage industry.
Source: Wikimedia Commons
Attribution: The Eyes Of New York
License: CC BY-SA 2.0

Consider the ongoing debate surrounding energy consumption, and, specifically, offshore drilling. In this case, the problems are oil shortages and consequent rising oil costs. Environmental groups and pro-business groups constantly compete to persuade policymakers to adopt solutions that do not endanger their own group's interests. Businesses and oil companies believe that rising fuel costs are *caused* by unreliable foreign oil sources, international conflict, taxes, and market manipulation. These groups argue that the key to energy independence is producing domestic oil through a variety of means rather than relying on foreign governments. Using economic data, pro-business and oil groups lobby to assure policymakers and the public that offshore oil drilling is safe and will provide a much-needed solution to the problem caused by external forces (Kilian, 2014).

4.4 AGENDAS AND AGENDA SETTING

Once a public problem has been identified, policymakers must choose to embrace that issue before a policy solution can be adopted. How does the problem get the attention of a policymaker? Why do policymakers pay more attention to some issues over others? Visit the website of any Congress member, and you will find a list of "issues" that are a priority for that policymaker. This list is called an **agenda**, and, whether implicitly or explicitly, every policymaker has one. Agendas include all the issues currently being discussed by the news media, interest groups, constituents, and the public-at-large. John Kingdon (1985) describes the agenda as "the list of subjects or problems to which government officials . . . are paying some serious attention at any given time."

The word "agenda" often invokes images of sinister plots, conspiracy theories, and corruption, but that is hardly ever the case. Instead, the agendas that we discuss in this chapter are simply plans of action or a list of topics being considered by the public and policymakers. Agendas can come in many forms, from an actual list of proposed bills to a series of principles, values, or beliefs that motivate citizens, organizations, and governments to act. Table 1 provides several examples of legislative agendas. Each policymaker has different priorities, and policymakers base those priorities on their personal interests and the needs of their home district.

Senator (A)	Congressman (B)	Congresswoman (C)
Virginia	Georgia	Minnesota
Consumer Protection	Agriculture	Immigrant Rights
Cyber Security	2nd Amendment Rights	Environmental Justice
Education and Workforce Training	Health Care Reform	Medicare for All
Infrastructure	Pro-Life	Worker's Rights

Table 4.1: Examples of Congressional Agendas
Source: Original Work
Attribution: Kimberly Martin
License: CC BY-SA 4.0

4.4.1 Agenda Levels

The public agenda includes a wide range of issues that may or may not be seriously considered by policymakers. The issues that currently occupy the agenda can be further organized into levels or categories that indicate how close they are to being acted upon by government. The first and broadest level of the agenda is the **agenda universe**. The agenda universe encompasses all the possible ideas that could be discussed or considered by government (Birkland, 2019). Almost any idea could be floating around in the agenda universe, although some ideas are more or less acceptable based on cultural norms. For example, in the U.S., topics such as child labor or anything overtly racist or communist are generally outside the realm of public consideration and are viewed as unacceptable solutions to public problems. Policy ideas like privatizing social security, allowing health care companies to reject people with preexisting conditions, outlawing firearms, open-borders, or even closed-borders, on the other hand, have recently been included in the agenda universe.

The next level of the agenda, the **systemic agenda**, includes "all issues that are commonly perceived by members of the political community as meriting public attention and as involving matters within the legitimate jurisdiction of existing governmental authority" (Cobb & Elder, 1983). Contrary to the agenda universe, the policies that make it onto the systemic agenda are those that could receive government attention or those that policymakers are willing to consider and address. Policies will not make it to the systemic agenda if government has no authority over that issue. For example, in 2016, Congress considered regulating the National Football League (NFL) in the wake of revelations about the dangerous effects of concussions on football players (Webster 2017). Ultimately, Congress's power over the NFL was called into question, and the issue lost its place on the systemic agenda.

While many policy goals may seem unachievable now, the ability of policy ideas to gain traction and move successfully through the agenda levels depends on support from policymakers and citizens. Rinfret, Scheberle, and Pautz (2019) describe the border between the agenda universe and systemic agenda as "porous," meaning that issues flow freely from one level to the next. Not only is the border porous but some issues move from one level to another as what was once unacceptable becomes acceptable. There was a time in U.S. history when the idea of women voting was unimaginable, as was school integration or same-sex marriage. Until 2010, most U.S. citizens opposed marijuana legalization. By 2018, though, 62% favored legalization (Pew Research, 2018), and, currently, sixteen states have legalized the drug for recreational use.

Policies do not have to be popular or free of controversy to make it onto the systemic agenda. Take, for instance, the universal healthcare proposal "Medicare for All." In the U.S., government-run or single-payer healthcare programs are viewed

> **Stop and Think**
>
> Identify an issue that never made it onto the public agenda. Why do you think this issue was not more successful?

as socialist. While Democrats favor "Medicare for All," the concept of socialized medicine is not as popular among Republicans (Silver 2019). Nevertheless, "Medicare for All" is a prominent fixture in the systemic agenda.

Policies that progress to the next level of the agenda are included in the **institutional agenda**. This level contains the "list of items explicitly up for active and serious consideration" (Cobb & Elder, 1983). Technically speaking, policy issues on the institutional agenda are those that make it into bill form and are assigned to a committee (Birkland, 2019).

While it may seem like an accomplishment for lawmakers to move potential policies into the realm of consideration, only 3% of originally proposed bills are enacted, and only 6% of resolutions are passed during any given Congress (govtrack.us). For example, environmental groups have been pushing Congress to pass legislation addressing climate change for years. In 2019, Senator Edward Markey (D) and Representative Alexandria Ocasio-Cortez (D) introduced the Green New Deal which they argued would curb the effects of climate change. The House of Representatives has conducted dozens of climate change hearings on the proposed legislation, although policies addressing this topic have yet to receive a vote in committee (Nawaguna, 2019).

Other policies have had greater success moving from the institutional to the final level of the agenda: the **decision agenda**. The decision agenda "describes those problems for which government is actively debating a solution and taking specific actions and making decisions, like taking a vote" (Rinfret et al. 2019). The policies at this level include bills or resolutions that are about to be acted upon by Congress or other government entities. For example, the CARES Act was an

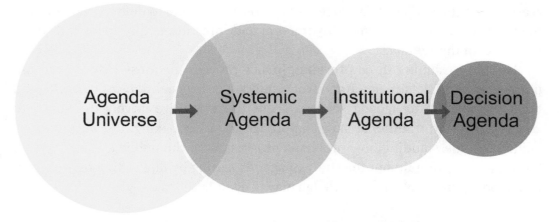

Figure 4.2: Agenda levels and sample policies.
Source: Original Work
Attribution: Kimberly Martin
License: CC BY SA 4.0

economic stimulus bill, passed through Congress with support from both parties, during the COVID-19 pandemic. The Act exemplifies a policy that was considered on the decision agenda.

4.5 GETTING IDEAS ON THE AGENDA – PREVAILING THEORIES

How and why do some issues move successfully through the stages of the agenda setting process while others are never considered? A few short years ago, some members of Congress made a significant push to eliminate the penny (C.O.I.N.S Act, 2017). What happened to that idea? In the 1970s, manufacturers and politicians floated the idea of converting measurements to the metric system. Only three countries in the world do not use the metric system: Myanmar, Liberia, and the U.S. (Marciano, 2014). Sounds interesting, so why were measurements never changed? The world is full of policy ideas that never happened and of those that captured attention but eventually lost their appeal. Ideas and policy issues are constantly gaining and losing importance on the public agenda.

The process of getting an issue recognized and placed on the agenda is called **agenda setting**. During the agenda setting process, groups compete to control the agenda and promote their issue as the most important among all other issues being considered. Groups also compete to keep issues off the agenda (Cobb and Ross, 1997). It is important to note that the number of issues that governments can address is finite. Think of the agenda setting process as a "bottleneck" with all ideas attempting to rush out at once, but only a select few are considered seriously. No government can address every problem when it arises. For this reason, internal and external forces continuously compete to define problems and to ensure that their problem gains traction and influence before making it to the final level of the agenda.

Here, we examine three prevailing policy process theories—elite theory and pluralism, multiple streams framework, and advocacy coalition framework—and their relationship to agenda setting. These theories were largely developed to add depth to the traditional stages approach to policymaking, but also serve as guides to understanding how problems progress onto the public agenda. In fact, these theories compliment the study of agenda setting by illustrating the role that institutions, interests, and knowledge play in agenda setting.

4.6 PLURALISM AND ELITE THEORY

The American government was founded on democratic principles that encourage open and accessible participation by all citizens. **Pluralism** follows the belief that everyone has "equal access to influence policymaking" (Dahl 1961; Rinfret, Scheberle, and Pautz, 2019); thus, anyone has the power to move public problems onto the agenda or, at the very least, attract the attention of policymakers who can. Competition still occurs between groups and individuals in the pluralist model, but many different actors have power; no single group dominates the decision-making process. Individuals and groups can also move freely into and out of the policy process, depending on whether their goals are met.

Contrast pluralist theory with **elite theory**, which suggests that only a few prominent elites have the power to influence policymaking. Elite theory asserts that regular citizens are uninformed and uninterested in public policy, leaving the elites of society, that is, politicians, businessmen, and the wealthy, in a position to control policy decisions (Mills, 1956). Policy, therefore, reflects not the demands of regular people but the values of elites.

> **Stop and Think**
>
> How does elite theory differ from pluralist theory? In your opinion, which theory better explains who has more power to set the agenda?

Elite theory implies that policy issues make it on the agenda from "inside" the policy process. For example, every few years, Congress discusses repealing the estate tax. According to the nonpartisan Center on Budget and Policy Priorities, the estate tax affects only .2% of all Americans, yet any proposed changes attract attention. The estate tax has provided a reliable source of revenue for the federal government for almost a century (Huang and Cho, 2017). For that reason, economists argue that eliminating the tax would cost the public billions, making the current budget deficit even worse. How does this issue nevertheless gain so much traction with policymakers? If elite theory is correct, it is because influential and wealthy individuals would benefit from a repeal of the estate tax. As members of an elite group, these individuals lobby from within the political system, using power and influence to prevent attempts to increase the estate tax from ever reaching the institutional agenda.

4.7 POLICY STREAMS AND "WINDOWS" OF OPPORTUNITY

John Kingdon was working on health care and transportation policy for the federal government in the 1970s and 80s when he observed a pattern in the way that topics came to the attention of policy makers. Kingdon proposed three "streams" that must unite for a "policy window" to open and place a potential policy on the public agenda. The model that Kindgon created, called the Multiple Streams Framework (MSF), continues to be an influential model in policy literature. While the MSF was primarily developed to better explain how policy problems and solutions attain prominence during the agenda setting process (Kingdon, 2011), MSF is also considered a stand-alone theory of policy making and often compared to the stages heuristic model discussed in chapter 3.

If the context aligns and a policy idea has support from policymakers, the issue is considered "ripe" for a policy solution (Kingdon, 2003; Stewart, Hedge, Lester,

2008). How do we know when a policy is "ripe?" John Kingdon (2011) argues that three conditions must be satisfied before an idea gains traction. He describes these conditions as the three "streams" of the agenda setting process: (1) the problem stream, (2) the policy stream, and (3) the political stream. If the conditions laid out in the various streams are met, a brief "window of opportunity" will open, and the policy has a greater likelihood of becoming law. However, policy windows only stay open for a short time: "If participants cannot or do not take advantage of these opportunities, they must bide their time until the next opportunity comes along" (Kingdon, 2003).

The **problem stream** is an event that changes our perception of a problem and indicates that something is wrong. For instance, employment rates may drop, crime rates increase, or doctors begin to notice a sudden increase in the number of people becoming sick from vaping. The statistical data connected to the previous examples are considered **indicators**. Extreme fluctuations in common indicators suggest that a problem is forthcoming, and government action may be necessary. For example, analysts in the financial sector began to see alarming trends in foreclosure rates that eventually led to the 2008 recession. In the early 2000s, doctors began to report an increase in deaths due to opioid addiction. In both instances, changes over time to financial and medical indicators resulted in increased attention from policymakers. In the case of the financial crisis, legislation was passed to regulate the banking industry.

Not every fluctuating indicator will lead to public policy. Often statistical changes go ignored or are not deemed significant enough for action. Instead, "interest groups, government agencies, and policy entrepreneurs use these numbers to advance their preferred policy ideas" (Birkland, 2018). Sometimes they are successful, and sometimes they are not. As mentioned, government simply does not have the ability to address every problem.

While indicators typically illustrate slow changes, **focusing events** are "sudden and rare events that spark intense media and public attention because of their sheer magnitude or because of the harm they reveal" (Birkland, 2018). Events such as the September 11 attacks, violent protests and rallies, a nuclear disaster, an oil spill, or an unexpected epidemic can all trigger action from policymakers. At the very least, such events cause public outcry and embolden the public to pay more attention to undiscovered issues.

When Hurricane Katrina made landfall as a category 5 hurricane in 2005, it quickly became apparent that all levels of government (local, state, and federal) were woefully unprepared for such levels of devastation. As a result of Hurricane Katrina, the Federal Emergency Management Agency (FEMA), along with state and local emergency services, have undergone numerous changes. New technology and procedures were adopted to quickly and efficiently con-

Stop and Think

Give an example of a focusing event. Did any significant policy change result from this focusing event?

nect state and local first responders. Also, Congress gave FEMA greater authority to move resources before a storm rather than wait until other government levels request aid (Roberts, 2017).

Kingdon's **policy stream** includes any proposals that have been developed to address a particular issue (Stewart et al., 2008). Customarily, the policy stream consists of a viable policy option or even concrete legislation, but it can also incorporate technology or even public perception. For example, immigration reform is a frequent topic on the public agenda. Immigration experts and lawmakers have considered various solutions to curb illegal immigration including building a wall on the southern border, reforming the Visa system, aiding South American countries to improve their economy and fight crime, and even closing the border or canceling such immigration programs as the Diversity Immigrant Visa. However, aside from efforts to obtain support from Congress to build a border wall, Congress has not proposed any policy options to reform the current immigration system. As the debate surrounding immigration reform has become exceptionally partisan in nature, proposed policy options are unlikely to gain support from both parties.

The final stage in the policy streams approach is the **political stream**. The political stream comes into play when electoral change or change in public opinion leads to reform. For instance, a change in political regime or increasing support for an issue can generate conditions favorable for policy change. President Trump came into office promising tax reform, including measures to simplify the tax code. With a Republican majority in both chambers of Congress, the President was able to pass the Tax Cuts and Jobs Act of 2017.

Likewise, changes in public opinion can also influence the political stream. Public support for same-sex marriage is a good example of public opinion galvanizing policy changes. A 2010 Gallup Poll found that only 44% of adults supported same-sex marriage. In roughly five years, the number of supportive adults increased from 44% to over 60%. Increased public support for same-sex marriage led to legalization in individual states prior to the Supreme Court ruling in *Obergefell v. Hodges* (2015) that expanded the right to all fifty states (Pew Research).

Do policymakers use public opinion to guide their decisions and actions? The rather complicated answer is, sometimes. For example, the public became outraged after it was revealed that migrant children were held without their parents in detention centers across the southern U.S. border. At the height of public controversy over child separations, polls from *CBS, CNN*, and Quinnipiac University found that 66% of Americans opposed the separations (Smith and

> **Stop and Think**
>
> Explain either marijuana legalization or universal health care using Kingdon's streams metaphor as a guide. If you do not think that a policy supporting one of these ideas is likely to pass, suggest which stream could be strengthened to increase the likelihood that the policy will pass.

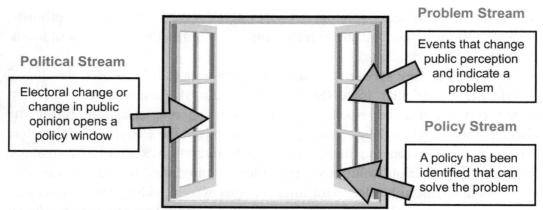

Figure 4.3: Kingdon's Policy Streams and Windows of Opportunity
Source: Original Work
Attribution: Kimberly Martin
License: CC BY-SA 4.0

Phillips, 2018). The combination of public outcry and negative public opinion led President Trump to sign an executive order that ended the practice of child separation.

Gerston (1997) argues that the *scope* and *intensity* of public support determine whether a policy issue comes to the attention of policymakers. When taking into account scope, policymakers consider how widespread the problem has become. According to Gerston, "If only a small percentage of the population is worried, then the issue will fail the scope test because of its inability to generate enough attention" (Gerston, 1997). This does not mean that a small group cannot get an item on the agenda; it simply means that issues that reach the broader public consciousness are more likely to attract immediate attention. Likewise, intensity refers to the strength and depth of reactions from the public. Is the public's response to a problem lukewarm and disinterested, or are protestors lining the streets and calling congressional offices? It will come as no surprise that the issue with protestors lining the streets will receive more immediate attention from policymakers.

Alternatively, many examples exist in which the scope and intensity of the American public's opinions on an issue were highly supportive yet Congress still failed to act. The ongoing debate surrounding gun control is one of those issues. A 2019 Gallup poll found that 63% of American adults believe that laws covering the sale of firearms should be "more strict." Moreover, policies such as universal background checks have garnered over 90% support; however, this support does not necessarily translate into actual policy (Cohn & Sanger-Katz, 2019).

Gerston (1997) also notes that intensity is not always enough to draw the attention of lawmakers. Sometimes the *duration* of the intensity determines whether a policy will make it onto an agenda. As with most focusing events, support for gun control measures increases after mass shootings (Gallup Poll, 2018). While support for stricter laws remains steady, after a shooting such as the one in Parkland, Florida, or El Paso, Texas, public support for new laws can spike by up to 20% (New York Times, 2019). However, public interest generally fades within a month of a mass shooting event (Parker et al., 2017). You will recall from earlier chapters, and your American government courses, that the policy process takes time and effort. If interest fades while legislation meanders through the process, it takes the pressure off policymakers to follow through with legislation that aligns with public opinion. Often interest groups and activists create strategies to maintain public pressure because they know that increased public support over long periods will more likely lead to success (Gerston, 1997).

Finally, *resources* determine whether an issue will generate more or less attention. Policy problems that cost more to fix will generate more attention than will less costly problems (Gerston, 1997). Consider the debates surrounding health care and education spending. Congressional proposals for universal health care or free college education are regularly met by critics who argue that the cost to implement these policies is simply too high. High costs do not automatically prevent policies from being enacted, but supporters will need to craft an argument that highlights the beneficial outcomes of the program over the costs. In the end, if a public problem receives widespread attention, generates an intense reaction, keeps the public's attention for a long period of time, and has identified resources to support a solution, the problem has a much greater chance of ending up on the agenda.

4.8 ADVOCACY COALITIONS

Sabatier and Jenkins-Smith (1993) developed the **Advocacy Coalition Framework** to explain policymaking and policy change over time. Advocacy coalitions consist of people "from a variety of positions (e.g., elected and agency officials, interest group leaders, researchers) who share a specific belief system— i.e., a set of basic values, causal assumptions, and problem perceptions—and who show a nontrivial degree of coordinated activity overtime" (Sabatier, 1988; Sabatier and Jenkins-Smith ,1993). The framework theorizes that competition between coalitions of actors—who advocate for their preferred solution to a public problem—is a common characteristic of the policy process. The ACF assumes that policies are made in an uncertain and ambiguous policy making environment with multiple actors and government levels involved, taking place over the course of many years, possibly decades.

The advocacy coalition framework was developed to inform the overall policy process, but many of its lessons apply to agenda setting. For instance, the framework centers on policymaking that includes many individuals, groups, and organizations. Policy change occurs when these groups work together to portray policy problems in a way that will increase the likelihood that they receive attention from policymakers. This feature of the advocacy coalition framework informs the agenda setting process through translation of public problems into policy solutions. According to Mintrom, "The quality of the collective interactions in the coalition and the coordination ability of those seeking to promote policy change greatly affect the likelihood that change will occur" (Mintrom, 2019). Thus, a variety of individuals and groups, with a persuasively defined problem statement and viable solution, are in a good position to capture the attention of policymakers and alter the agenda.

Earlier in the chapter, we discussed the importance of group competition to define a problem and bring the problem to the attention of policymakers, thereby setting the agenda. Consider the debate on gun laws that ensues after each mass shooting in the United States. Sabatier (1998) remarked that pro- and anti-gun coalitions are particularly suited to the parameters of the ACF as "these subsystems seem to be characterized by well-defined coalitions driven by belief-driven conflict . . . at multiple levels of government."

After mass shootings, coalitions—comprising citizens, interest groups, policymakers, and other government actors—act quickly to identify and define the cause of mass shootings. The resulting definitions are guided by the coalition's core values. Sabatier (1998) explains that the ACF takes into account policy core beliefs and values which "represent a coalition's basic normative commitments and causal perceptions across an entire policy domain or subsystem. ACF assumes that policy core beliefs are the fundamental 'glue' of coalitions." As an example, groups supporting gun control argue that the problem results from the easy availability of guns and, in particular, of automatic weapons with high capacity magazines. On the other hand, pro-gun groups identify mental health, improper parenting, and even video game violence as the cause of gun violence. Powerful gun rights lobbyists and the history of the Second Amendment are unique to American culture. We see, therefore, that values and belief structures are among the many influential factors that set the context for what advocacy coalitions will and will not consider for inclusion on the public agenda.

4.9 WHO SETS THE AGENDA?

As discussed in chapter 3, numerous groups and individuals play a role in the policy making process. However, agenda setting is only one step in the process, and the actors who influence agenda setting are not always the same as those who influence, for instance, policy implementation. Who specifically has the *power* to influence the agenda and persuade policymakers to fight for solutions to public problems? Power is a complex topic, to say the least, but many groups and even individual citizens can acquire the power to set the agenda. We discuss those actors and their role in detail in this section.

4.9.1 Subgovernment

Douglass Cater (1964) coined the term "subgovernment" to describe three sets of actors in the agenda setting process: (1) congress members on key committees, (2) bureaucrats overseeing the issue, and (3) interest groups with a vested interest in the policy outcome. It is no secret that influential congress members can use the committee process to direct a policy debate and set the agenda by choosing to take on certain issues over others. Congress members are responsible for developing policy solutions and translating those solutions into legislation. Policy ideas often come directly from legislators and represent ideas or issues that are important to them and their constituency. Newly elected policymakers often have their own ideas for bills. They are motivated by experiences and observations, along with expertise in specific fields. For instance, one House member from South Carolina has a degree in ocean engineering. He frequently proposes bills opposing offshore drilling and promotes environmental policies that protect the coastline and natural resources. Not only do elected leaders have expertise in specific fields, but bureaucrats from executive agencies also have the type of in-depth knowledge necessary to identify a problem and get the attention of policymakers who can address that problem.

4.9.2 Bureaucrats

Bureaucrats, that is, nonelected government officials, occupy varying levels of involvement in the agenda setting process. Many have the power to set the agenda and are deeply involved in this step of the policy process. While bureaucrats do not typically dominate the agenda setting process from beginning to end (Kingdon, 1995), the level of bureaucratic influence depends on the way issues are framed and defined (O'Toole, 1989) and the amount of control that the president, Congress, and the courts exert over the agency (Golden, 2003). Most people assume that important policies originate in Congress or with the president, but Potter (2019) estimates that nearly 90% of law is created by administrative rules issued by federal or even state agencies. The National Highway Traffic Safety Administration (NHTSA) employs a number of auto safety specialists and engineers who research the causes of injury and death from auto accidents. This research often results in traffic and safety policies when bureaucrats determine that, for instance, a new technology would decrease fatalities (Golden, 2003).

Countless stories attest to bureaucratic intervention in the agenda setting process. For example, the Environmental Protection Agency (EPA) works with outside interest groups to drive the environmental agenda. Many of the policies they introduce become law or such administrative regulations as those setting fuel standards, regulating air quality and emissions, determining which pesticides are safe, or ensuring clean drinking water. The Department of Housing and Urban Development recently proposed controversial changes to the Fair Housing Act (O'Donnell, 2019); also, the Department of Health and Human Services proposed a rule to revise protections for transgender patients under the Affordable Care Act (ACA or Obamacare) (Abutaleb, 2019). Most, if not all, of these policy changes originated from unelected bureaucrats working within their specific career fields.

Figure 4.4: The Environmental Protection Agency (EPA) sets regulatory standards for air quality and emissions.
Source: Wikimedia Commons
Attribution: Steven Greenwood
License: Public Domain

4.9.3 Interest groups

Interest groups clearly play an integral role in the agenda setting process by lobbying policymakers to propose bills and presenting research and other evidence that supports their policy goals. According to the Center for Responsive Politics, lobbying groups spend upwards of $3 billion a year to influence public policy. Much of their time is spent on seeking support or encouraging opposition for existing bills, essentially taking a reactive approach to the actions of policymakers. A great deal of their effort also goes toward persuading policymakers to embrace issues that the group would like to see on the agenda. Halpin and Fraussen (2019) argue that interest groups are highly strategic in taking a proactive approach to the agenda setting process. Interest groups commonly set goals based on the group's values and priorities and develop a plan to progress these goals. Groups start with a list of issues that promote their interests. They then refine that list into a smaller list of priorities. From the list of priorities, interest groups concentrate on the issues they believe have a legitimate shot at success (Halpin 2015).

Earlier in the chapter, we discussed Kingdon's (1984) multiple streams model of agenda setting. In many ways, this model helps explain the actions of interest groups who are highly sensitive to the presence of an "open window." While interest groups are less likely to spend their time promoting a policy that is unpopular or overlooked, they will invest their "time, political capital, energy and other resources" when they see that a policy window of opportunity has opened. For example, the highly influential pro-Israel interest group, the American Israel Public Affairs Committee (AIPAC), lobbied against the Iran Nuclear Treaty throughout President Obama's time in office. They were unsuccessful until the political stream opened when Donald Trump was elected president. Once AIPAC had a more sympathetic ear in the White House, they were able to push the issue back onto the agenda and successfully lobbied the new president to withdraw from the agreement (Demirjian & Morello, 2015). As this example illustrates, the most effective interest groups are prepared to "seize the moment," as windows do not remain open indefinitely (Kingdon, 1984).

4.9.4 Media

The media's ability to set the agenda is perhaps one of the most controversial processes in politics. Thomas Dye (2013) writes that the media is both a "player and referee in the game of politics" by reporting information to the public and participating in the competition to control the agenda, potentially opening up windows of opportunity for policy change. The media has immense power to set the public agenda by determining which issues are considered newsworthy. Editors, producers, reporters, and columnists have the power to guide what people talk and think about. Media effects on the agenda setting process include the following: (1) the ability to identify issues and set the agenda, (2) the ability to influence viewpoints and opinions on policy issues, and (3) the ability to influence the behavior of citizens and policymakers (Dye, 2013).

As an example, chances are you have heard about lead-contaminated water in Flint, Michigan, but did you know that more than 5,000 U.S. water systems— serving 18 million people across the country—violated EPA lead standards in 2016 (Layne, 2018)? Aging infrastructure has caused lead levels to increase in drinking water. The cost to replace old lead pipes has been estimated at several trillion dollars. Why is there no public outcry? Only a handful of news organizations have reported on EPA lead standard violations, and none of these stories was featured prominently enough to capture the public's attention (Ganim 2016, Layne, 2018). If the media had chosen to feature the lead issue more prominently, they could have interviewed citizens and public officials, run stories more frequently, and/or brought in experts to discuss the dangers of contaminated pipes during a twenty-four-hour broadcast program. The media could urge citizens to call their representatives, creating a sense of urgency and alarm among the public. If they so choose, the media has the necessary power and influence to bolster public awareness, get the attention of policymakers, and place this issue on the agenda.

Finally, the media influences how people see an issue through a process known as **framing**. With framing, how a topic is presented to the audience affects the choices people make about how to process that information. For example, before the 2016 election, media outlets reported on possible conflicts of interest between

Hillary Clinton's campaign and her husband's non-profit organization, the Clinton Foundation. When this story broke, *CNN's* headline described the accusations as "ridiculous," while the *Fox News* story on that same topic suggested the Democratic Party's silence about the allegations implied they were true. Both *CNN* and *Fox News* were attempting to frame the story and influence public opinion. The previous example is not an isolated event. A quick look at competing news sources illustrates the power of the media to frame how the public, and even policymakers, think about specific issues. Fortunately, the public is not powerless in their ability to influence the agenda.

4.9.5 Citizens

Earlier in the chapter, we mentioned the power of public opinion and how increases in support for an issue can push that issue onto the public agenda. For instance, an increase in support for the decriminalization of recreational marijuana was the driving force behind change in some states. We also mentioned that the intensity of public outcry over an issue could lead to policy change. For instance, outrage over police shootings led to such policy changes as police officers wearing body cameras. These examples have one thing in common: they were the result of a large group of people changing their opinion or sparking widespread anger. This concept might lead some to believe that issues can only be added to the agenda if large groups band together to force change, but that is simply not the case. Students and everyday citizens often believe that they do not have direct access to their representatives. This could not be further from the truth. Not only can individuals meet with and propose policy ideas to their representatives but citizens can take more strategic steps to get the attention of their representatives and push for policy ideas to be added to the agenda. In fact, many policy ideas originate directly from constituents.

Schattschneider (1960) writes that "the group that successfully describes a problem will also be the one that defines the solutions to it, thereby prevailing in the policy debate." There are strategies that individuals and groups can use to define a problem and catch the attention of policymakers. Even every-day citizens have the power to move problems onto the agenda. For instance, have you ever been confronted with an issue at your university or in your community and thought, "I should do something about this?" Once you determine that your problem can be addressed through government intervention, use your anger or concern as a catalyst for action. According to Graham and Hand, "Your first step in launching a citizen initiative is to understand and clearly state the problem you want to fix" (Graham and Hand, 2008). A useful problem definition should be both specific and realistic. We would all like for our community, state, country, or world to be a better place, but such a statement simply does not provide enough specificity to incite action from policymakers. More precise problem definitions might include statements such as the following:

- Vacant and run-down properties in my neighborhood are bringing down property values and pose a safety hazard.

- Small businesses in my area cannot afford to pay for health insurance for employees.

- Fish from my local river are no longer edible due to pollutants.

- High school graduates should be required to take a course on budgeting and life management skills (aka "Adulting").

Graham and Hand (2008) argue that the problem should be framed in a broader context. For example, say that your car was broken into and your belongings stolen while you were sleeping one night. If one individual's car was broken into, others have likely had the same experience. It is also possible that these types of crimes have been happening for a while. Instead of going to local policymakers and complaining about one car break in, you should define the problem as a broader concern about public safety throughout the neighborhood.

If the goal is to make a change, the definition of the problem should also identify a desired outcome. Too often, we hear interest groups and concerned citizens declare that they would like to see change, but what might that change look like? If, for example, you are passionate about preventing human trafficking, instead of approaching policymakers asking them to develop a policy to prevent trafficking, consider lobbying state representatives to pass legislation that protects migrant workers with temporary visas from predatory trafficking businesses. Specifying the desired outcome in this way is more likely to lead to positive results.

Define the problem in public terms (Graham and Hand, 2008). No matter the target audience, you want your problem to be memorable. People have short attention spans, and policymakers are no different. Define your message in a brief but memorable way. The most effective messages mention the goal of the potential policy, and a "catchy" slogan can help create a memorable impression. In 2018, for example, Florida included an initiative on the November ballot that would amend the state constitution to allow felons to vote after they serve their time in prison (Replogal and Licon, 2019). The amendment was nicknamed the "Second Chances" amendment, and supporters of the measure wore t-shirts with the slogan, "Let My People Vote." This type of creative marketing led to a successful public campaign that resulted in the amendment passing.

Earlier in the chapter, we mentioned the importance of defining the problem when attempting to influence the public agenda. Once citizens have defined the problem in a compelling and planned way, they must focus on gathering research to support their claims and bolster their credibility before confronting policymakers. Citizens should understand every aspect of their chosen issue. This may mean wading through newspapers, public opinion polls, and other sources that give historical context to the topic (Gerston, 1997). Citizens also must identify who in government can fix their problems. If a student is concerned about the nutritional value of lunches served at their school, it would not make sense for them to appeal to the mayor or the town sheriff who has no control over what is served in schools. Citizens must understand who can solve their problems and focus their attention by going directly to that source. Citizens should also make a plan to build coalitions and solicit the help of the media and other stakeholders when necessary (Graham & Hand, 2010). While this list is brief and does not include the complicated nuances that inevitably arise from citizen action, the goal here is simply to encourage students to use their power as citizens to make necessary changes in their community.

Finally, one of the most direct and effective methods for citizens to influence the agenda is through voting. Casting a vote for the policymaker who most directly aligns with your preferences can result in greater emphasis on those issues (Abbe et al., 2003). Lupia (1992) notes that citizens have even more success at setting the agenda through voting in states that offer direct voter initiatives and referendum. Regardless, voting for policymakers who embrace the same values and policy preferences as their constituents can directly influence the issues that appear on the public agenda.

4.10 CASE STUDY: SETTING THE HEALTH CARE AGENDA

President Obama signed the Patient Protection and Affordable Care Act (ACA), also known as *Obamacare*, in March of 2010. Health care reform was a priority for President Obama, even before taking office. On the campaign trail, he often promised to make access to quality and affordable health care the centerpiece of his policy agenda. Shortly after his inauguration, President Obama made good on his promise to elevate health care reform to the top of his policy agenda by working with Congress to develop a plan. Passage of the ACA came after a year of tense and grueling debate to determine what the new law should include and who would be affected.

How did health care reform end up on the agenda? Bill Clinton had campaigned on the promise of reforming health care more than a decade earlier. In fact, universal healthcare was the linchpin of Clinton's first-term agenda. Opposition to Clinton's plan came from conservatives and, most notably, the healthcare industry, which made a concerted effort to rally public opposition to the plan. Support from Democrats was tepid, and, instead of rallying behind Clinton's proposal, several Democrats submitted plans of their own. Eventually, Democrats and even some Republicans settled on a compromise bill, but that bill never received the support it needed to become law (Clymer, 1994). Health care reform was not seriously considered again in the U.S. until President Obama took office in 2009.

Public support for government-provided health insurance decreased immediately following President Clinton's attempt to pass a universal health care policy and remained low until Clinton left office. By 2009, the Gallup Organization reported that the American public named access to health care the most urgent healthcare concern facing the country (Saad, 2010). Over 44 million

Americans lacked health insurance before the ACA (Kaiser Family Foundation). Additionally, Americans had become increasingly supportive of government intervention in health insurance reform during the ten years prior to the passage of the ACA, primarily viewing health care coverage as a responsibility of the government (Conway, 2013). While public support for government intervention ranged between 54 and 64%, that number fell to less than 50% as the ACA made its way through the political process. Even with a Democratic majority in the House and Senate, reform proved to be more complicated than planned. Republicans and even some Democrats opposed health care reform. As political and public support began to dwindle, President Obama decided to address Congress and the American public directly to sell his plan to fix the nation's health care system. President Obama used the "bully pulpit" as a tool to advocate for his agenda and, to some degree, was able to change public perception of the plan. Fahmy et al. (2013) found that the "more speeches that President Obama gave on the health care act in any given month, corresponded with an increase in the positive tone of articles discussing this bill." Likewise, data showed that the public was less supportive of the ACA during months when President Obama did not give any speeches promoting the ACA.

Framing the health care debate. Once President Obama took office, health care reform moved quickly from the agenda universe to the decision agenda. Recall that this stage in the agenda setting process comprises all the issues that the government is actively debating and considering. The decision agenda is a precarious stage for a controversial policy. At any point, a strategic and cunning opposition group could frame the policy in a way that resonates with the public, thwarting plans for bill passage. Framing influences the way the public understands an issue and can lead to higher levels of support or opposition. Much to Obama's credit, he remained the top news source throughout the entire debate process, which allowed his arguments to frame the policy in a more positive light (Fahmy, 2013).

Support for a policy often hinges on media support, which, in turn, influences public opinion on an issue. The media framed the health care debate in one of several ways. The first and most dominant frame focused on the politics or policy implications of health care reform. More specifically, media framing concentrated on controversial claims made by opposition groups, such as assertions that the policy would result in "death panels." The second most utilized frame defined health care reform as an economic transaction, either as an economic necessity or as an overly expensive economic policy. Conservative news sources argued that the plan would increase the national debt and cause damage to the economy. Competing interests argued that there were economic benefits to insuring all Americans and advocated for a plan that prohibited private insurance. However, the media spent little time explaining the implications of the proposed reforms or what changes might mean for Americans (Fahmy, 2013).

The amount of media effort spent on reporting the controversial and political aspects of the policy, such as the intense conflict between Republicans and Democrats, led many to argue that had the media focused on other aspects of the plan, public opposition would not have been a concern: "For without the public being on board with specific . . . policies, it is quite difficult for any public health program to achieve its maximum health impact" (Parekh, 2017, Gollust et al., 2017). The focus on partisanship, affordability, and even misinformation likely contributed to lower levels of overall support for the ACA. Interestingly, polling data suggests that some aspects of the ACA were attractive to both Republicans and Democrats, such as allowing young adults to stay on their parent's plans until they are 26 or no care exclusions for preexisting conditions. Had these messages been tailored to the correct audience, one could speculate that the general public may have been more receptive. When promoting an agenda, the goal of policymakers should always be to match audiences with the most suitable message.

Multiple Streams. John Kingdon (2011) argues that three conditions must be satisfied before a policy idea gains traction. He describes these conditions as the three "streams" of the agenda setting process: (1) the problem stream, (2) the policy stream, and (3) the political stream. If the conditions laid out in the various streams are met, a brief "window of opportunity" will open, and policy has a greater likelihood of becoming law. Before passage of the ACA, more than 44 million people were without health insurance; the largest groups of uninsured Americans were low-income and people of color. Several health indicators revealed that even those who were insured spent a high percentage of their income on medical care. While it was clear that the poor lacked adequate coverage, inadequate coverage had begun to affect the middle class as well (Garfield, Orgerea, and Damico, 2019). Couple this information with an American public that was open to government intervention and had increasingly viewed access to quality care as the most pressing health care issue facing the country (Gallup Poll, 2009). It is no wonder that policymakers were convinced that the problem stream was satisfied. One could also argue that the policy stream was in play. Massachusetts enacted a similar program three years prior that included an individual mandate and an insurance exchange. While President Obama had a basic plan going into office, his administration used the Massachusetts plan as a guide during the policy development phase. Furthermore, the ACA incorporated components—the individual mandate, for example—that had already been promoted by conservative groups. The final stream of Kingdon's model was complete when President Obama was elected into office, along with a Democratic majority in Congress that supported sweeping health care reform. Opposition groups were relentless, using strategic framing in an attempt to change the debate and alter the public's perceptions. In the end, though, each policy stream aligned, opening a brief window of opportunity that led to passage of the ACA.

4.11 CRITICAL THINKING QUESTIONS – AGENDA SETTING AND THE ACA

- Explain the focusing events and indicators that pushed health care reform onto the public agenda. What arguments or information do you think had the greatest influence on the American public?

- What framing techniques did opposition groups use to remove health care reform from the agenda?

4.12 CHAPTER SUMMARY

In this chapter, we discuss how public problems are identified and then included on the agenda. Policy agendas can be formal lists of bills that a policymaker is attempting to pass into law or a less formal collection of topics that are of interest to the policymaker. The agenda setting process encompasses a complex set of steps and actors. Elites, bureaucrats, the media, interest groups, and even citizens all have the ability to set the agenda. Agenda setting is one of the most important steps in the policy process, as this is where public problems are identified, solutions are defined, and topics gain and lose importance among policy makers and the public.

4.13 KEY TERMS

- Advocacy Coalition Framework
- Agenda
- Agenda Setting
- Agenda Universe
- Causality
- Decision Agenda
- Elite Theory
- Focusing Events
- Indicators
- Institutional Agenda
- Pluralism
- Policy Stream
- Political Stream
- Problem Stream
- Systemic Agenda
- Framing

4.14 REFERENCES

Abbe, Owen, Goodliffe, Jay, Herrnson, Paul, & Patterson, Kelly 2003. "Agenda Setting in Congressional Elections: The Impact of Issues and Campaigns on Voting Behavior." *Political Research Quarterly*, 56(4), 419–430.

Abutaleb, Yasmeen. 2019. "U.S. Health Agency Proposes Reversing Obamacare Transgender Protections." *Reuters,* May 24, 2019. Retrieved from https://www. reuters.com/article/us-usa-healthcare-transgender/u-s-health-agency-proposes-reversing-obamacare-transgender-protections-idUSKCN1SU1IF.

Anderson, James. 2015. *Public Policymaking*. Stamford, CT: Cengage Learning.

Beisser, Sally R. 2008. "Unintended Consequences of No Child Left Behind Mandates on Gifted Students." *Forum on Public Policy Online* No2.

Birkland, Thomas. 2019. *An Introduction to the Policy Process: Theories, Concepts, and Models of Public Policy Making*. New York, NY: Routledge.

Bragdon, J., and Marlin, J. 1972. "Is Pollution Profitable?" *Risk Management* 19: 9-18.

Brandt, Allan. 2012. "Inventing Conflicts of Interest: A History of Tobacco Industry Tactics." *American Journal of Public Health* 102 (1): 63-71.

Cater, Douglass. 1964. *Power in Washington: A Critical Look at Today's Struggle to Govern in the Nation's Capital*. New York, NY: Random House.

Clymer, Adam. 1994. "National Health Program, President's Greatest Goal, Declared Dead in Congress." *The New York Times*. Sept 27 1994. Retrieved from https://www. nytimes.com/1994/09/27/us/health-care-debate-overview-national-health-program-president-s-greatest-goal.html?pagewanted=all

Cohn, Nate, and Margot Sanger-Katz. 2019. "On Guns, Public Opinion and Public Policy Often Diverge." *New York Times*. Retrieved from https://www.nytimes. com/2019/08/10 /upshot/gun-control-polling-policies.html.

Conway, Bethany Anne. 2013. "Addressing the 'Medical Malady:" Second-Level Agenda Setting and Public Approval of 'Obamacare." *International Journal of Public Opinion Research*. 25(4): 535-546.

Demirjian, Karoun, and Carol Morello. 2015. "HOW AIPAC Lost the Iran Deal Fight." *The Washington Post*. Sept 3 2015. Retrieved from https://www. washingtonpost.com/ news/powerpost/wp/2015/09/03/how-aipac-lost-the-iran-deal-fight/

Dye, Thomas. 2013. *Understanding Public Policy*. Boston, MA: Pearson.

Edelman, Adam. 2018. "Trump Signs Order Stopping his Policy of Separating Families at Border." *NBC News*, June 20, 2018. Retrieved from https://www.nbcnews.com/ politics/ immigration/trump-says-he-ll-sign-order-stopping-separation-families-border-n885061

Fahmy, Shahira, Christopher McKinley, Christine Filer, and Paul Wright. 2013. "Pulling the Plug on Grandma: Obama's Health Care Pitch, Media Coverage & Public Opinion." *Advances in Journalism and Communication*. 1(3): 19-25.

Ganim, Sara. 2016. "5,300 U.S. Water Systems are in Violation of LEAD Rules." *CNN*. Jun 29 2016. Retrieved from https://www.cnn.com/2016/06/28/us/epa-lead-in-u-s-water-systems/index.html

Garfield, Rachel, Kendal Orgera, and Anthony Damico. 2019. "The Uninsured and the ACA: A Primer - Key Facts about Health Insurance and the Uninsured amidst Changes to the Affordable Care Act." The Kaiser Family Foundation. Retrieved from https://www.kff.org/report-section/the-uninsured-and-the-aca-a-primer-key-facts-about-health-insurance-and-the-uninsured-amidst-changes-to-the-affordable-care-act-how-many-people-are-uninsured/.

Gerston, Larry. 1997. *Public Policy Making: Process and Principles*. Armonck, NY: M.E. Sharpe.

Golden, Marissa. 2003. Who Controls the Bureaucracy? The Case of Agenda Setting. National Public Management Research Conference, 9 October 2003, Georgetown University.

Gollust, Sarah, Laura Baum, Jeff Niederdeppe, Colleen Barry. 2017. "Local Television News Coverage of the Affordable Care Act: Emphasizing Politics over Consumer Information." *American Journal of Public Health*. 107(5): 687-693.

Guilfoyle, Christy. 2006. "NCLB: Is There Life Beyond Testing?" *Educational Leadership* 64 (3): 8-13.

Halpin, D. 2015. Interest group "policy agendas": What are they? And how might we study them? In Cigler, A. J., Loomis, B. A., Nownes, A. N. (Eds.), *Interest Group Politics*. Washington, DC: CQ Press.

Halpin, D., & Fraussen, B. (2019). Laying the Groundwork: Linking Internal Agenda-Setting Processes of Interest Groups to Their Role in Policy Making. *Administration & Society, 51*(8): 1337–1359.

Jenkins-Smith, Hank, and Sabatier, Paul. 1994. "Evaluating the Advocacy Coalition Framework." *Journal of Public Policy*, 14(2): 175–203

Kilian, Lutz. 2014. "Oil Price Shocks: Causes and Consequences." *Annual Review of Resource Economics* 6: 133-154

Kingdon, John. 1995. Agendas, Alternatives and Public Policies. NY: Addison-Wesley. (2nd edition).

Kingdon, John. 2003. *Agendas, Alternatives, and Public Policies*. New York, NY: Longman.

Layne, Rachel. 2018. "Lead in America's Water Systems is a National Problem." *CBS News*. Nov 21 2018. Retrieved from https://www.cbsnews.com/news/lead-in-americas-water-systems-is-a-national-problem/

Lewis-Beck, Michael, William Jacoby, Helmut Norpoth, and Herbert Weisberg. 2008. *The American Voter Revisited*, Ann Arbor, MI: University of Michigan Press.

Lupia, Arthur. 1992. "Busy Voters, Agenda Control, and the Power of Information." *The American Political Science Review, 86*(2), 390-403.

Marciano, John. 2014. "Why Won't America Go Metric?" *Time*. Dec 15 2014. Retrieved from https://time.com/3633514/why-wont-america-go-metric/

Mills, Wright. 1956. *The Power Elite*. London: Oxford University Press.

Mintrom, Michael. 2019. *Public Policy: Investing for a Better World*. New York, NY: Oxford University Press.

Nawaguna, Elvina. 2019. "Democrats Appear Stymied on a Top Priority: Climate Legislation." *Roll Call*, July 18, 2019. Retrieved from https://www.rollcall.com/ news/ congress/democrats-appear-stymied-on-a-top-priority-climate-legislation

Nelson, Barbara. 1984. *Making an Issue of Child Abuse*. Chicago, IL: University of Chicago Press.

O'Donnell, Katy. 2019. "HUD to Propose More Hurdles to Prove Housing Discrimination. *Politico*, July 31, 2019. Retrieved from https://www.politico.com/story/2019/07/31/ hud-prove-housing-discrimination-1629826.

Osland, Joyce. 2003. "Broadening the Debate: The Pros and Cons of Globalization." *Journal of Management Inquiry*, 12 (2): 137-154.

O'Toole, Laurence. 1989. *Handbook of Public Administration*. San Francisco, CA: Jossey Bass.

Parekh, Anand. 2017. "Public Health Communications: Lessons Learned for the Affordable Care Act." *American Journal of Public Health*. 107(5): 639–641

Parker, Kim, Juliana Horowitz, Ruth Igielnik, Baxter Oliphant, and Anna Brown. 2017. "America's Complex Relationship with Guns: An In-Depth Look at the Attitudes and Experiences of U.S. Adults." *Pew Research Center*. Retrieved from https://www. pewsocialtrends.org/2017/06/22/americas-complex-relationship-with-guns/

Potter, Rachel. 2019. *Bending the Rules: Procedural Politicking in the Bureaucracy*. Chicago, IL: University of Chicago Press.

Pozen, Robert. 2019. "Repeal or Replace: Two Opposing Estate Tax Proposals." *The Hill*. Feb 25 2019. Retrieved from https://www.brookings.edu/opinions/repeal-or- replace-two-opposing-estate-tax-proposals/

Replogel, Joshua and Adriana Gomez Licon. 2019. "Florida Felons Rejoice After Regaining Their Right to Vote." *AP News*. Jan 8 2019. Retrieved from https://www. apnews.com/a0086670a6df42c9a3d2857d1606e027.

Rinfret, Sara, Denise Scheberle, Michelle Pautz. 2019. *Public Policy: A Concise Introduction*. Thousand Oaks, CA: CQ Press.

Roberts, Patrick. 2017. "5 Things That Have Changed About FEMA since Katrina – And 5 Things That Haven't." *The Conversation*. Retrieved from http://theconversation. com/5-things-that-have-changed-about-fema-since-katrina-and-5-that- havent-83205

Rochefort, David, and Roger Cobb, eds. 1994. *The Politics of Problem Definition: Shaping the Policy Agenda*. Lawrence, KS: University Press of Kansas.

Sabatier, Paul. 1988. "An Advocacy Coalition Framework of Policy Change and the Role of Policy-Oriented Learning Therein," *Policy Sciences* 21 (2): 129-168.

Sabatier, Paul, and Hank Jenkins-Smith, eds. 1993. *Policy Change and Learning: An Advocacy Coalition Approach*. Boulder, CO: Westview Press.

Sabatier, Paul. 1998. "The Advocacy Coalition Framework: Revisions and Relevance for Europe." *Journal of European Public Policy*, 5(1): 98-130.

Schattschneider, E.E. 1960. *The Semi-Sovereign People: A Realist's View of Democracy in America*. New York, NY: Holt, Rinehart, and Winston, Inc.

Silver, Nate. 2019. "Medicare For All Isn't That Popular – Even Among Democrats." *FiveThirtyEight*, July 25, 2019. Retrieved from https://fivethirtyeight.com/features/medicare-for-all-isnt-that-popular-even-among-democrats/

Smith, David, and Tom Phillips. 2018. "Child Separations: Trump Faces Extreme Backlash for Public and His Own Party." *The Guardian*, June 19, 2018. Retrieved from https://www.theguardian.com/us-news/2018/jun/19/child-separation-camps-trump-border-policy-backlash-republicans

Stewart, Joseph, David Hedge, and James Lester. 2008. *Public Policy: An Evolutionary Approach*. Boston, MA: Thomas Wadsworth.

Stimson, James, Michael Mackuen, and Robert Erikson. 1995. "Dynamic Representation." *American Political Science Review* 89 (3): 543–565.

Stone, Deborah. 1997. *Policy Paradox: The Art of Political Decision Making*. New York, NY: W.W. Norton.

Webster, Lynn. 2017. "Congress Needs to Recognize the Seriousness of Football-Related Brain Injuries." *The Hill*, August 9, 2017. Retrieved from https://thehill.com/blogs/pundits-blog/healthcare/345864-congress-needs-to-recognize-the-seriousness-of-football-related

5

Policy Design and Formulation

5.1 CHAPTER OBJECTIVES:

- Describe the processes leading to public policy formation.
- Summarize policy goals, outputs, and outcomes.
- Recognize trade-offs between policy goals.
- Apply the various policy tools used to formulate successful policy.
- Compare and apply decision making models to real-life policy issues.

In chapter 4, we discussed how policy makers, interest groups, and even everyday citizens have the power to affect the public agenda. Once a policy idea has made it onto the agenda, more work must be done to move the policy through the next step in the political process. Specifically, the policy must be articulated and methodically designed for consideration by policymakers. Policy design is the practice of creating a policy response to a public problem (Peters, 2018). Birkland (2019) defines **policy design** as the "process by which policies are designed, through both technical analysis and the political process." Policy design is the policymaker's attempt to define policy goals and to connect those goals to instruments or tools that will result in achievement of those goals (Howlett, 2010). The result of policy design is the physical development of a policy proposal, or blueprint, that will eventually take the form of either a bill, regulation, or executive order. Most policy proposals in the design phase include the following elements: goals, causal models, tools, information about the target population, and a description of how the policy will be implemented (Birkland, 2019).

As an example, consider the legalization of recreational marijuana, also discussed in chapter 4. The states that have legalized marijuana did so with differing goals in mind, but, in general, most sought to decrease incarceration rates, cut out potentially dangerous "middle-men," and create new revenue streams. Supporters of legalization created convincing causal stories demonstrating a link between marijuana arrests and the cost of those arrests on society. Once the policy made its way onto the systemic agenda, it was not enough for policy makers to simply declare marijuana legal. There were many details to consider when designing the policy. These details had to address such questions as, who can purchase marijuana and how much can an individual possess? Will age limits be placed on those who can purchase the drug? Who can grow and sell marijuana and related products? How will those who break the rules be punished? What happens to prisoners currently in jail for marijuana possession? Are offenders with misdemeanor marijuana possession convictions eligible for expungement, or will felony charges be reduced to misdemeanors? This simple example demonstrates the complexity of the policy design and formulation process. Throughout this chapter, we will discuss the intricacies of the process and even suggest ways for students to practice policy design and formulation.

5.2 MEETING GOALS

The first step in policy design is to start with the *goal*. By goal, we mean the desired outcome of a policy. At this point in the process, individuals or groups have already identified a problem, *indicators* or *focusing events* have put the spotlight on that problem, the public has supported a solution, and policymakers are prepared to act. But what do policymakers expect to happen once the policy is implemented? Is the goal of the policy to eliminate a problem? Perhaps, the goal is to keep the problem from getting worse.

Stone (2002) describes public policy as the "rational attempt to attain objectives and goals." Objectives are "specific, quantified targets that represent steps toward accomplishing goals" (Worth, 2016). Public policy goals incorporate four major concepts: equity, efficiency, security, and liberty (Stone, 2002). To note, while these concepts are referred to as goals, they are perhaps more appropriately described as policy justifications or even criteria for evaluating policy efficacy. What's more, while equity, efficiency, security, and liberty appear to be straightforward concepts, in truth, they have the potential to complicate political debates and introduce ambiguity and doubt. Each concept is continuously redefined and constructed by society. Take equity, for example; our perceptions of this term continually evolve. Throughout much of American history, black and female citizens were not treated with equity. Expanding fair and equitable treatment to these groups was not a priority for many elected officials. Now, unequal treatment plays a central role in policy debates. Policymakers use these terms to frame their positions while attempting to convince others that their interpretation best fits the broader concepts. As Stone writes, "In a paradoxical way, the concepts unite people at the same time as they divide" (Stone, 2002).

5.3 EQUITY

Distributive policies, those that distribute such goods or services as wealth, education, or health care, should be designed with fair and reasonable outcomes as

Figure 5.1: Equity plays a central role in current policy debates.
Source: Wikimedia Commons
Attribution: Elvert Barnes
License: CC BY SA 2.0

the ultimate goal. Stone (2002) uses a cake as an example to illustrate the difficulties associated with achieving truly equitable polices. In her metaphor, Stone offers her students chocolate cake. However, we'll imagine that on one afternoon a southern favorite, the key lime pie, appears in a public policy class at the local university. Everyone in class likes key lime pie, and, at first, the class agrees that the most equitable way to serve the pie would be to divide it into equal slices and distribute those slices to each person in class. Inevitably, students begin to object to the equal distribution of the pie. One student concludes that because she did not have breakfast that morning and is extremely hungry, she deserves a larger slice of the pie. Another student notes that he has two children and will need a large enough slice to share with them. Still another student, who is nontraditional, notes that he is the oldest in the classroom and suggests they divide slices according to age, with older students receiving a larger slice. At that point, the instructor points out that she has more years of formal education and deserves a larger slice of the pie. The instructor also mentions that, before class, she and five students contributed money to the "pie" fund. Once enough money was collected, two other students drove to the bakery to buy the pie and bring it back to class. The other ten students in the class did not use any of their own money to purchase the pie, nor did they expend any effort to retrieve the pie from the bakery. Surely, the students and instructor who either bought the pie or delivered it deserve larger slices.

This simple pie scenario is a metaphor for understanding the process of designing policy with the explicit goal of providing fair and equitable distribution of a good or service. All students began the class happily agreeing that everyone should have an equal slice, but several quickly challenged that design. Take, for instance, the student who felt that older students should have a larger slice or the instructor who felt that her education entitled her to a larger slice. Both arguments base distribution on rank and merit. The student and instructor expect unequal treatment for people at different ranks; those who are younger or less educated will receive less. Distribution by rank is a central principle that guides how society allocates rewards. We expect to be rewarded upon reaching a higher level through more years of experience or an advanced degree. As Stone notes, "our fundamental belief that rewards such as jobs...and pay should be distributed according to achievement, competence, and other measures of past performance goes hand in hand with a belief in the legitimacy of rank-based distribution" (Stone, 2002).

In a classroom exercise, students work through a scenario requiring they decide who is accepted into a hypothetical law school. Students first learn that less than 3% of the practicing attorneys in the state where the law school is located are African American. Students also receive demographic information about students currently attending the law school: a majority are Caucasian. Students then receive a list of law school applicants. The list includes each applicant's gender, race, GPA, and LSAT score; minority applicants have slightly lower GPA's and LSAT scores. The class must then decide who to accept and who to reject. Most classes, with some exceptions, accept the applicants with the highest GPAs and LSAT scores. They justify their choices as being based on merit. This exact argument applies to affirmative action policy, which was conceived as a group-based remedy for violations of merit- and rank-based distribution. Affirmative action raised such questions as, is there a justifiable reason for students from underrepresented groups being accepted? Can universities prove a compelling interest, or should admissions be awarded strictly on merit? On the one hand, supporters of affirmative action point out that minority groups have been denied admissions based on discriminatory practices. Affirmative action policies, therefore, offer ways to ease the racial disparities present at some universities, similar to those present at the hypothetical law school. Opponents argue that affirmative action is a form of reverse discrimination, by which students who may be more qualified are passed over in favor of diversity, resulting in a loss of benefits for majority groups.

Returning to the pie example, the students who chipped in to pay for the pie and those who took time out of their day to travel to the bakery illustrate another common equity argument. When designing new distributive programs, policymakers must decide who receives the benefit and how much of the good or service the group receives. Stone (2002) writes that people will agree that distributions are just if the process for acquiring those goods is deemed fair. For many distributive policies, including welfare, health care, and education, the process of determining who receives the benefit is often considered unfair. Opponents commonly argue that they should not have to work hard and pay into a system that gives more significant benefits for unequal effort.

5.4 EFFICIENCY

Most Americans have heard or possibly uttered the phrase, "government should run more like a business." The implicit assumption here is that, unlike government, businesses are efficient and competent. Unsurprisingly, because many policymakers value cost-effective, small government solutions, they focus much of their effort on efficiency as a policy goal. **Efficiency** is the act of "achieving an objective for the lowest cost" or gaining the most output for a given level of input, or even getting more of something for less (Birkland, 2019). Frequently, policymakers must determine how to use the scarce resources available to them so as to achieve the desired outcomes. Stone argues that rather than being a policy's ultimate goal, efficiency is a means for helping policymakers attain more of the outcomes they value. If you think about it, we use efficiency to judge whether many of our daily activities are worth our time. Efficient people get a lot accomplished in a short period of time. Policymakers argue about efficiency when discussing a variety of public issues: military spending, health care, immigration, voting, and even foreign policy. Perhaps no policy is more controversial than government efforts to achieve efficiency through public school funding. Supporters argue that schools do not have the necessary resources to improve student performance, while opponents argue that increased funding does not equate to increased achievement. Specifically, opponents argue that increased funding will not lead to greater efficiency.

Getting the most for less money, time, or effort is an intuitive way to judge policy options because "everyone would like to attain something of value in the least costly way" (Stone, 2002). That is why government agencies initiate a bidding process before deciding which private company will provide government services. The Government Accountability Office (GAO) releases a yearly report that identifies waste and federal program duplication. A recent report found, for example, that the Department of Energy could avoid spending billions on radioactive waste cleanup by developing a strategy to improve hazardous waste cleanup (GAO, 2019).

Americans commonly think of government expenses as wasteful or fraudulent, taking resources away from more worthy causes or taxpayers in general. In fact, the argument against inefficiency is so rewarding that policymakers who disagree with the substance of a policy will find its argument about limited resources and waste to be the most successful. While inefficiencies do occur in government, the decision to either support or oppose a policy based on efficiency is more often political than economic. Take, for instance, the economic arguments against the Affordable Care Act (ACA) when first debated in Congress. Opponents disagreed with the substance of the policy but found the arguments against the policy cost or the likelihood of fraud were more compelling (Fahmy, 2013).

5.5 INPUTS, OUTPUTS, AND OUTCOMES

Policymakers can and do improve efficiency in public programs by applying measures that were once thought of use only to private businesses. Increases in productivity are useful to both the public and private sectors and can be determined by measuring policy outputs in relation to the resources used to achieve those outputs. Does productivity always lead to efficiency in public policy? Policymakers can apply what scholars refer to as a results chain logic model as a guide to identifying the components of a successful policy. A results chain model is a "linear process with inputs and activities at the front and long-term outcomes at the end" (Funnell & Rogers, 2011). Developing these benchmarks makes it much easier to assess whether a policy is implemented correctly, is meeting desired goals, or needs adjustments or changes.

Inputs are resources dedicated to a policy or public program. These could be money, staff, facilities, time, or anything of value that provides the foundation for the policy to function. Students can learn to apply the results chain logic model through the input outcomes "sandwich" example. For this example, imagine you are hungry and that your goal is to construct a sandwich. Inputs would include anything you might use to make a sandwich: two slices of bread, cheese, turkey, lettuce, tomato, and/or mustard. Activities are actions taken by implementers and policymakers to meet policy objectives. Activities are what implementors do with the inputs to fulfill the policy's mission. The activities required to make a sandwich are straightforward. Put one piece of bread on a plate and add the desired amount of toppings, then add the remaining piece of bread. **Outputs** are "the immediate, easily measurable effects of a policy, whereas **outcomes** are the ultimate changes that a policy will yield" (Tieghi, 2017). Outcomes also convey the benefits the policy is designed to deliver. The immediate, and obvious, outputs of sandwich making are that a sandwich is now made. The outcomes are where the actual effects of creating a sandwich begin to take shape. Now that a sandwich is created, it can be eaten, and the person who eats it is no longer hungry; because their body receives nourishment, they can continue their day. The **impacts** are the higher-level goals and long-term consequences of a policy that lead to measurable improvements in people's lives. The person who has eaten the sandwich can now contribute more fully to society or excel at their job or school because they are no longer hungry. Perhaps they will go on to produce new or innovative policies themselves now that their bodies are nourished and minds have been fed. And to think, all these amazing things happened because someone decided to make a sandwich!

This humorous example is simplistic in its design but a valuable way to emphasize the results chain process. Students can easily apply the results chain to their own experiences. For instance, most students would claim the outcome of their college career is to graduate and obtain a well-paying job. The logic model in Figure 5.2 outlines that process. Inputs are all the resources the student puts into obtaining a college degree, such as tuition, books, and housing costs.

Students must attend class and study to receive good grades and prepare for the workforce. The outcome may be to graduate, but the impact of years of hard work is much broader. Students who graduate from college are more likely to achieve financial stability, gain a sense of personal satisfaction and happiness, and become a more productive citizen overall (Carnevale et al., 2016).

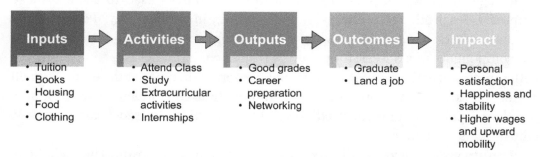

Figure 5.2: Results Chain Logic Model Applied to College Degree Attainment
Source: Original Work
Attribution: Kimberly Martin
License: CC BY SA 4.0

The results chain can be applied to a wide range of policy issues. Designing efficient public policy requires the same level of planning and dedication as that used to create the results chain model. However, policymakers often make the mistake of focusing on outputs rather than on outcomes or impacts. Outcomes, as the most immediate result of a policy, are easy to identify. Despite their similarities, outputs and outcomes are not identical. For instance, policymakers might be intent on lessening crime in a city. Local leaders often discuss the need for additional police officers as a means of achieving this goal. By adding more officers to the force (input), the output would be a higher number of officers patrolling the city. However, having more officers does not necessarily mean the outcome will be less crime or the impact will be a safer city. Perhaps the city has an unusually high rate of gang violence, or, because few job opportunities exist, most citizens live in poverty. If that is the case, the city will need to change their inputs to meet stated goals.

5.6 SECURITY AND LIBERTY

The U.S. Constitution ensures rights to "life, liberty, and the pursuit of happiness" for its citizens. Just how much responsibility the government has to ensure life, liberty, and happiness forms the basis for an enduring and controversial debate about security. **Security** is defined in a multitude of ways: humans can be economically, physically, or even psychologically secure. One could argue that we must feel secure in order to pursue happiness. We often think of security as a feeling of personal safety, that is, feeling we are safe from bodily injury or attempts to harm our property. Safety almost always equates with security, so the pursuit of safety has become a major concern for policymakers.

For example, should the government regulate food and drug production, car and airplane manufacturers, or mitigate environmental hazards to keep us safe? When citizens cannot trust the source of their food or are unsure if the car they drive uses faulty parts, or cannot fish out of concern for water pollution, they are less likely to pursue the liberties, freedoms, and happiness espoused by the Constitution.

The founders agreed to add a Bill of Rights to the Constitution to protect citizens from unnecessary intrusion from a powerful central government. These protections gave the American people the freedom to pursue whatever interests lead to their pursuits of happiness. The Bill of Rights not only protects citizens against government but also lays out a blueprint for the protection of those accused of a crime. In theory, these two concepts exist in harmony; citizens enjoy both security and the liberty to pursue their interests. Problems arise in instances when it becomes clear that citizens must make some concessions to realize either complete security or complete liberty. The truth is that security comes with a cost, which often is liberty. This paradox is one modern philosophers and writers have examined at length.

Philosophers such as Thomas Hobbes, John Locke, and Jean-Jacque Rousseau wrote extensively about social contract theory. In a civil society, a social contract is necessary because a person's obligations depend on an agreement among all citizens to form their society. Imagine a time before there were laws or governments. Philosophers argue that in this *state of nature*, devoid of rules or oversight, humans did whatever they wanted and would fight for limited resources and power. In this society, no one was secure. If someone needed food and another person had a cow, the first person would use their brute strength to force the second to give up the animal. Hobbes reasoned that people would rather live in a civilized society than amidst the chaos associated with the state of nature. Rational people, he argued, would give up some of their freedom for the sake of acquiring greater security. The result would be the establishment of a theoretical social contract that forms the rules around which society is based as well as a civil government to enforce them (Hobbes, 1651).

The social contract requires citizens to surrender or limit those liberties they believe are necessary for the government to maintain order and security. "Under such system, citizens retain considerable rights and privileges of citizenship" until they have breached the laws agreed upon through the social contract. When laws are breached, "individual liberties can be taken in order to make all of us more secure" (Birkland, 2019). We can find countless examples of policies that force citizens to choose between security and liberty. Many people would prefer not to wear seat belts in a car, but the law says that we must in order to ensure the safety of drivers and passengers. Before September 11, the federal government did not require security screenings at airports. Anyone planning a flight would simply retrieve their ticket and walk directly to the boarding gate. Now travelers must remove specified items of clothing as well as display before a line of strangers, x-ray images of their suitcase's contents in order to safely board a plane. Violence on public school campuses has resulted in metal detectors and, in some cases, additional school resource officers. Law enforcement frequently wiretaps the telephone conversations of suspected terrorists. Average citizens, therefore, have surrendered their rights to private phone conversations to ensure safety.

The tradeoff works the other way as well. Not uncommonly, people reject greater security for more liberty. Destructive hurricanes and rising sea levels are a threat to coastal communities. The safest action people could take would be to cease living in coastal areas, but the likelihood of anyone giving up that liberty is doubtful. We have discussed the gun control debate at length in this textbook. On one hand, supporters of gun restrictions argue that ownership should be limited to increase safety. Opponents argue that the liberty to own a firearm must be protected, even if security is compromised. These differing points of view illustrate the compromises and controversy associated with policies that address security and liberty.

5.7 DEVELOPING CAUSAL STORIES

Establishing causality during the design phase is imperative for the long-term success of a policy. Deborah Stone (2002) divides causal stories into four separate categories: accidental, intentional, mechanical, and inadvertent. *Accidental* causes refer to problems caused by accident, fate, or luck, such as natural disasters. Fires, hurricanes, floods, and sometimes ill health are consequences of phenomena that are not the fault of any person or group. In direct contrast with accidental causes, *intentional* causes can be attributed to a person or group who knowingly caused harm. Companies that chose to increase profits rather than control pollution (Bragdon & Marlin, 1972) or cigarette manufacturers who sold tobacco products after receiving evidence that cigarettes were harmful (Brandt, 2012) are examples of intentional causal stories.

Mechanical causes "include things that have no will of their own but are designed, programmed, or trained by humans to produce certain consequences" (Stone, 2002). First, mechanical causes exist because the actions of a person are guided indirectly by an "intervening agent," or people are acting automatically to carry out the will of others. This type of action is often attributed to bureaucratic officials who, instead of using their own discretion, will follow a strict interpretation of a

> ### Stop and Think
>
> Think of a public problem that you care about. Develop a causal story to explain what causes the problem. Do you think your causal story will be accepted by society? Why or why not? How might groups who oppose your causal story argue against your position?

policy. Mechanical causes can also be attributed to mechanical errors. In 2018, the state of Hawaii sent out a terrifying emergency alert message warning of an incoming ballistic missile threat. The threat was not real; the emergency alert was sent by accident, but it caused a wave of panic among residents and tourists alike. While the direct cause of the mistake was human error, officials blamed its delayed correction on a flaw in the alert system (Nagourney et al., 2018).

Causal stories also include *inadvertent* causes or the unintended consequences of well-meaning policies. Policymakers often believe that a particular policy will address the actual cause of a problem, but the result is an unintended consequence. For example, proponents of globalization and free trade argue that policies promoting these practices will lower costs and foster competition, thereby encouraging economic advancement in developing countries. As an unintended consequence, though, some free trade policies led to an increase in the wealth gap, exploitation of workers and the environment, and companies moving their operations to other countries (Osland, 2003). The goal of the No Child Left Behind Act of 2001 (NCLB) was to close achievement gaps and provide students with a fair and equal opportunity for a quality education. The emphasis placed by NCLB on bringing all students up to general competency levels in reading and math resulted in a decrease in funding for programs for gifted education programs (Beisser, 2008), and on "teaching to the test," marginalizing such subjects as art, history, and music (Guilfoyle, 2006). When designing policy, policymakers attempt to anticipate unintended consequences to the best of their ability. Of course, it is impossible to anticipate every consequence, but creative and critical thinking about policy outcomes can mean the difference between success and failure.

5.8 ESTABLISHING CAUSALITY

Causality is critical in the policy design process because establishing causality helps policymakers demonstrate how the effort expended affects a specific outcome. Think of the causal model as you might a formula: "If we do X, then Y will definitely happen." Causal stories can be simple; for example, "if I spill my drink on my lap, my pants will be wet," or "if I adopt another cat from the animal shelter, my mother will be angry." In each case, action results in an easily identifiable reaction. By applying these examples to public problems, though, we see that reactions may or may not be easy to identify. Consider the opioid addiction crisis. In order to solve the problem of opioid addiction, policymakers must create a causal link between the crisis and the reasons why the crisis developed. At one time, prescription pain pills were only available to cancer patients, and now one might argue that easy availability of prescription pain pills caused increases in addiction. The Centers for Disease Control reports that drug overdose deaths involving prescription opioids rose from 3,442 in 1999 to 17,029 in 2017. These figures correspond with a more aggressive marketing strategy among pharmaceutical companies in the late 1990s, who misrepresented the safety of prescription pain pills by assuring doctors that their patients would not become addicted (Center on Addiction).

Once a real cause and effect relationship has been established, policymakers can then develop a clear description of the problem and propose a solution. This is not a simple task—policy solutions are complex. Sometimes policymakers can an-

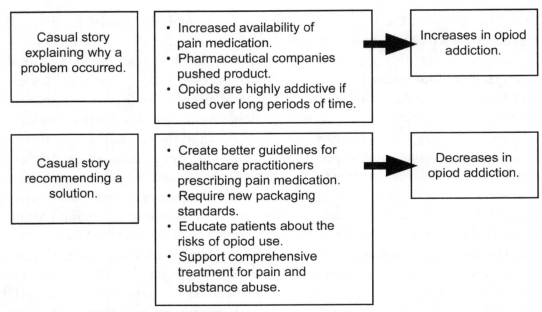

Figure 5.3: Creating Causal Stories to Solve Policy Problems
Source: Original Work
Attribution: Kimberly Martin
License: CC BY-SA 4.0

ticipate the consequences of their actions, and sometimes they cannot. Developing an accurate causal story requires exploring the root cause of an issue thoughtfully. Public problems are often symptoms of what is lying below the surface. Anyone developing a causal model must first identify the factors that contribute to the emergence of a problem and then treat the source of those problems using available options. The following are basic steps for establishing causality.

1. Demonstrate that the cause happened or will happen before the effect and rule out other plausible alternative explanations. The Insurance Institute for Highway Safety (IIHS) successfully made the case to Congress that lowering speed limits on highways would increase safety. When establishing causality, it is essential to rule out other cause and effect relationships. For instance, the condition of highways or driver distraction could all lead to decreased safety. Consequently, the IIHS did their research and compared outcomes before and after lower speed limits took effect in certain cities. They found that lower limits lead to a significant decline in speeding tickets and collisions (2019).

2. Demonstrate a relationship between two concepts. The causal model formula stated that "if we do X, then Y will happen." If you observe that whenever X is present, Y is also present, and that whenever X is absent, Y is also absent, then a relationship between the two concepts is confirmed. In the previous speed limit example, IIHS researchers were able to prove that when lower speed limits took effect (X), fewer speeding tickets and accidents occurred (Y). Without lower speed limits, drivers continued to speed and get into accidents.

5.9 POLICY FORMULATION AND DECISION-MAKING THEORIES

Policy formation is the act of developing alternatives for managing public problems on the policy agenda (Dye, 2013). It is the stage in the policy process where "pertinent and acceptable courses of action for dealing with a public problem are identified and enacted into law" (Anderson, 1990). As we have discussed in previous chapters, public problems are not easily defined, and solutions are numerous. Policymakers must often choose between many options to solve a problem. The act of choosing between alternatives is, at its core, decision making. Here we present several of the most well-known models of decision making.

5.10 RATIONAL COMPREHENSIVE MODEL

The American public would like to think that our representatives make rational policy decisions. The **rational comprehensive model** assumes that decisions are made after an individual rationally considers all options while estimating the trade-offs between costs and benefits. This model of decision making typically includes some combination of the following steps:

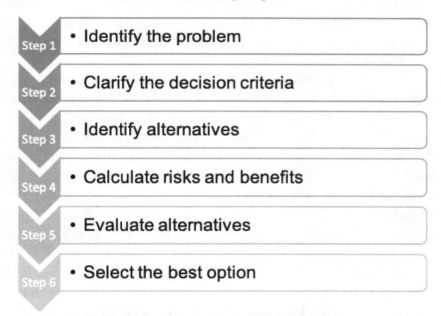

Step 1 • Identify the problem

Step 2 • Clarify the decision criteria

Step 3 • Identify alternatives

Step 4 • Calculate risks and benefits

Step 5 • Evaluate alternatives

Step 6 • Select the best option

Figure 5.4: Rational Comprehensive Model Decision Making Steps
Source: Original Work
Attribution: Kimberly Martin
License: CC BY-SA 4.0

Proving that you have a problem worthy of government action requires evidence in the form of data collection, indicators, or focusing events. Sometimes identifying a problem is relatively easy. Take, for example, the high cost of student loan debt. The U.S. Department of Education reported that outstanding student loan debt topped $1.4 trillion in 2018, and the average student owed $29,200. These changing indicators are clear; loan debt is increasing. Furthermore, the effects of student loan debt can be seen in the economy. Young people are delaying homeownership, marriage, and family to pay off their loans (Hembree, 2018). In this case, the problem is clear; student loan debt is crippling individuals and the economy.

Next, we need to choose the variables that will help us evaluate options. In other words, clarify the decision criteria. What goals, values, or objectives will guide you as a decision maker? Determining what criteria is relevant and what is not usually depends on individual values and beliefs. For instance, say that you believe a college education is a necessity that has become far too expensive for the average person. Often, the only way a young person can afford that necessary degree is by taking out student loans. At this point, you have already identified values and beliefs that will guide your decision. First, college is necessary, and, second, it is too expensive for the average person. By extension, if someone wants to better themselves through attaining a college degree, their ability to pay for it should not be a barrier to that decision.

Step 3 in the rational model requires policymakers to identify alternatives. If your decision criteria necessitates access to a college degree, the alternatives that you choose will also encompass those values. For example, many policymakers and candidates for public office have proposed policies that would deliver a free college education. Others have proposed canceling student debt up to a certain amount or eliminating debt entirely.

If you value a college degree for everyone who chooses to pursue one, your alternatives will include a list of proposals similar to those mentioned above. If you believe that college is a choice and choosing not to go to college is a viable option or that students should not rely on government to pay off their debts, you will likely choose different alternatives. Perhaps your options will include holding colleges accountable for lowering the cost of tuition or educating borrowers about job prospects and starting pay for degree programs.

Once you have identified all alternatives, calculate their risks and benefits. Is one alternative likely to yield better results but is far too expensive to consider? Will specific options yield unintended consequences? As an example, if we choose to cancel student loan debt, how much will it cost taxpayers? Is this a sustainable option and will eliminating student debt help us reach the policy goal? Once the risks and benefits of each option have been established, move to step 5 where decision makers will measure each alternative against the other, comparing and evaluating their advantages and disadvantages. Finally, after each alternative is evaluated, the decision maker "chooses the alternative that maximizes the attainment of his or her goals, values, or objectives" (Stewart, Hedge & Lester, 2008). The result of this process should be a rational decision that is both efficient and achieves the desired goal.

Like most theoretical models, the rational comprehensive model is not immune to criticism. Many criticisms stem from the assumptions implied by the model. The first assumption is that decision makers can define a problem and identify all aspects of it; for example, think about how difficult it is to identify the root cause of crime. Is crime a direct result of environmental factors, such as poverty, unemployment, and low educational attainment? Is crime a result of societal and political factors, such as discriminatory policies or systemic racism? Alternatively, is crime caused by individuals with a tendency toward violence, alcohol and drug abuse, etc.? Unless decision makers can genuinely identify what causes a problem, they will be unable to identify and evaluate alternative solutions.

Second, the rational comprehensive model assumes that decision makers have complete knowledge of the alternatives for dealing with a problem and that it is "possible to predict the consequences with complete accuracy" (Stewart, Hedge, Lester, 2008). In truth, neither policymakers nor researchers will ever have complete information or be able to predict consequences with perfect accuracy. Decision makers can predict some outcomes, but policy making is inherently a "trial and error" process.

Herbert Simon (1947, 1956) famously wrote that rational behaviors are an unrealistic description of the decision-making process. Instead, Simon argued that people are more likely to "satisfice," which is a term derived from the terms *satisfy* and *suffice*. In his acceptance speech for the Nobel Prize in Economics, Simon explained that "decision makers can satisfice either by finding optimum solutions for a simplified world, or by finding satisfactory solutions for a more realistic world." While he preferred to call this approach satisficing, what he described is what economists now refer to as bounded rationality. The central argument of bounded rationality is that no one makes completely rational decisions. We can easily observe this concept in real world situations. For instance, while policy makers may believe they are behaving rationally, they have actually developed short cuts or rules of thumb that help them make simplified and quicker decisions. The outcome of bounded rational decision making may not be optimal, but it is good enough.

Finally, even the most intelligent decision makers fall prey to their own self-interest. The greatest barrier to rational decision making is often human nature. Decision makers, especially in politics, often inevitably make decisions based on their own goals rather than on serving the greater good. Moreover, the rational decision-making process assumes there is only one decision maker, which is rarely the case. Multiple groups and many people often develop policies. Imagine considering the preferences of not one person but a group when deciding which alternative to choose.

5.11 INCREMENTALISM

Incrementalism occurs when policies are formulated to continue previous policies or make gradual changes to existing policies over time rather than developing new policies from scratch (Lindblom, 1959). With incrementalism, existing policies or programs are the basis for new policies. The pro-life movement provides a relevant example of incremental policy making. After *Roe v. Wade* (1973) made abortion legal in the U.S., the pro-life movement began to pass laws at both the state and federal level that "chipped away" at abortion law. While pro-life advocates realized they might not be able to overturn *Roe v. Wade (1973),* they recognized that incremental changes were a viable strategy. When the Supreme Court ruled on *Planned Parenthood v. Casey (1992),* the ruling opened the door for state and federal laws that would outlaw partial-birth abortions or require minors to get parental approval, enforce a 24-hour waiting period, or require a woman to view ultrasound pictures. This ruling resulted in a slow, but effective, plan to place greater restrictions on abortions.

Why might decision makers choose incremental policy instead of sweeping change? They might be unable to pre-dict the consequences of each policy option. If a significant number of "un-knowns" come to light during policy development, decision makers may opt for a more conservative approach. Pre-

> **Stop and Think**
>
> Do policymakers use the rational comprehensive model or incremental model more frequently? Reinforce your argument with a real-world example.

vious policies may prove to be effective or popular, so very few to no changes are necessary. In a pluralist political system, the government finds it easier to continue existing programs to satisfy a need or a demand than to engage in the complicated process of developing policies "from scratch." Gradual change gives the target audience more time to change their behavior. Decision makers therefore will engage in incremental policy making because it "reduces conflict and is politically expedient" (Stewart, Hedge, Lester, 2008).

The drawbacks to incremental decision making are that it does not account for dramatic shifts in policy. While an argument can be made that most policy change occurs incrementally, focusing events and other incidents often lead to policy change. Additionally, incrementalism does not explain such government efforts at long-range planning as the Iran Nuclear Deal or the Paris Climate Agreement, which were both meant to satisfy long term security and environmental goals.

5.12 GARBAGE CAN MODEL

The "**garbage can model**" of decision making offers a radical departure from the familiar rational approaches. Instead of well-planned decision making, this model assumes that decision making is irrational and uncertain, therefore resulting in conflict over goals and ambitions. In this case, "Policymaking becomes an expressive forum where policymakers 'act out' social and political agendas that are largely unrelated" (Stewart, Hedge & Lester, 2008). With the garbage can model, policymakers are disconnected and operate independently. The phrase "herding cats" comes to mind when reflecting on this model. The garbage can model's chaotic nature makes it difficult to solve problems, and the problems that are solved are only resolved by chance. Opportunities to develop solutions are treated like garbage cans. That is, many problems and solutions are thrown into the process at once without meaning or organization, like garbage in a can (Cohen, March, Olsen, 1972).

Recall from chapter 4 that problems must first be identified and then defined and understood before a solution can be pursued. A primary feature of garbage can decision making is that it often results in unnecessary solutions. Known as the *organizational garbage*, situations arise in which a solution seeks a problem rather than using the logical problem/solution decision structure. For instance, a group of legislators in Florida proposed a bill that would ban hydraulic fracturing, better known as *fracking*. Fracking is a process where liquid is blasted underground at high speeds to release oil or gas. Fracking has been known to cause air and water pollution, oil spills, and even earthquakes. As it turns out, no developers or oil companies have engaged in fracking operations in Florida for years (Blackmon, 2019). Critics argue that this is an example of a solution seeking a problem. They argue that if there is no fracking occurring in the state, then legislation is unnecessary.

> **Stop and Think**
>
> How might the garbage can model explain how environmental policy is made in the U.S.?

5.13 POLICY TOOLS

What is the most effective way to persuade you to do something? Are you more likely to change your behavior if there is a punishment for not acting, or would you prefer a reward for action? Policymakers have similar options at their disposal that they can use to create a desired outcome. **Policy tools** are "elements in policy design that cause the target audience to do something they would not do otherwise or with the intention of modifying behavior to solve public problems or attain policy goals" (Schneider & Ingram, 1997). Policymakers can choose between several elements when deciding between policy tools. This is not to say that policies cannot utilize multiple policy tools—they can and do. Instead, it emphasizes the importance of choosing the most effective and feasible political tool when designing policy. This process might mean that more than one tool is necessary to create effective legislation.

The two most common types of policy tools utilize either coercive or non-coercive measures. **Inducements** are options for changing people's behavior through rewards or punishments, sanctions, and incentives (Stone, 2002). What motivates humans to act or not to act? Knowledge of a penalty or the promise of a reward are proven methods for encouraging behavior changes. You may have heard the phrase "carrot or the stick." This phrase aptly describes the process of applying a reward or punishment to encourage a desired behavior.

More coercive policies are successful, but "considerable resources must be devoted to providing the coercion needed to create compliance" (Birkland, 2019). For example, the ACA required all Americans to purchase health insurance (individual mandate). Taxpayers could choose not to purchase insurance, but the penalty for noncompliance was a fine. When the individual mandate penalty was in effect, the Internal Revenue Service (IRS) would check the information provided by taxpayers with information reported by health insurers. Those who did not pay health insurance paid the fee. Other examples are fines for violating regulations or policies that withhold a service for the sake of compliance. Parking tickets, "sin taxes" on alcohol or nicotine products, or jail time for drug use are all punishments meant to discourage specific behaviors.

Non-coercive policies are easier to administer and require less oversight and enforcement, but their success varies based on assumptions about how people will react. Tax credits for families who outfit their homes with solar panels are a popular inducement. In fact, most tax credits are an incentive to produce a desired outcome. Taxpayers are eligible for tax credits for paying student loan interest or investing in business expenses or childcare. Other incentives include farm subsidies that ensure farmers will continue to farm even when they have unprofitable years. The government also awards small business loans and student loans to encourage people to open small businesses and attend college.

Facts are non-coercive policy tools that rely on persuasion to encourage behavioral changes. Facts do not necessarily provide a direct reward or punishment. Instead, the aim is to change people's perceptions of the world and, thus, their behavior. As Stone writes, "Persuasion... rests on giving people information and letting them make up their own minds" (Stone, 2002).

> **Stop and Think**
>
> Are coercive or non-coercive policy tools more effective? Strengthen your argument with an example of a policy that utilizes coercive or non-coercive measures.

Perhaps no better example of using facts as a policy tool exists than the rise of the anti-smoking movement. Studies, beginning in the 1940s and 50s, linked cancer with smoking, and several nonprofit organizations began public relations campaigns to educate the public about the risks. The government did not seriously intervene until years later (primarily due to pressure from the tobacco industry), but when they did, education proved key to changing the public's perception (Yale University Library). Who could forget the Drug Enforcement Agency's attempts to educate the public on the consequences of drug use in their "Just Say No" campaign and the U.S. Forest Service's campaign to prevent forest fires with their declaration that "Only you can prevent wildfires"?

As mentioned, policies can utilize more than one tool to ensure success. Often multiple policy tools are applied, as in the case of drug prevention policies. Policymakers have both strengthened the penalties for drug possession and attempted to educate the public about the dangers of drug use. Policy tools

Figure 5.5: Education is key to changing the public's perception of a problem. Smokey the Bear reminds citizens that "only you can prevent forest fires."
Source: Wikimedia Commons
Attribution: National Agricultural Library
License: Public Domain

also say a lot about politics and the assumptions made about the population that the policy targets. For instance, policymakers have enacted drug tests for welfare recipients (sanctions for low-income populations) and prescription incentive programs for Medicare recipients (incentives for the elderly).

Inevitably, the decision to choose one policy tool over another is a matter of feasibility. What sanctions or incentives does government have the resources to implement, and what tools better suit the target population? Consider educators who often cite the lack of parental involvement as a contributing factor for failing school systems. What resources does the school district have, and what tools can be used to encourage parents to increase involvement in their child's school

activities? Schools could propose a penalty when parents fail to participate in school events, or they could offer incentives, such as services and events that bring parents into the school. The penalty might be useful if parental involvement is extremely low and the school has the ability to enforce the penalty. On the other hand, if the school district has the ability to provide incentives, using those techniques could set a more conciliatory tone and encourage voluntary involvement.

5.14 ACTORS IN POLICY DESIGN & FORMULATION

Numerous government actors are involved in the policy design and formation process. Policy design and formulation occurs in government agencies, the executive and legislative branch, and even originates with interest groups and think tanks. Each actor plays a different role in the process: providing research and expertise to develop a policy, lobbying policymakers for specific language to include in the policy, and listening and acting on behalf of constituents. As we will see in the following section, bureaucrats, interest groups, and think tanks, rather than elite politicians, commonly play a significant role in policy development.

5.14.1 Government Agencies

Career bureaucrats working in government agencies play a critical role in the policy process. They help set the agenda, formulate, implement, and even evaluate policy. Many bureaucrats have been involved in policymaking for years and therefore have more professional expertise and knowledge in their specified field than do elected policymakers. During policy formation, government agencies provide research and other information to policymakers in Congress and the executive branch. This information often becomes the basis for future legislation. Agencies also provide Congress with information about the effectiveness of previous policies to ensure that inefficiencies are avoided in future legislation. For example, the Government Accountability Office (GAO) completed a study on the long-term health of the American economy. They concluded that current levels of public debt are unsustainable and suggested several changes to spending and revenue policy that would put the economy on a sustainable path (Dodaro, 2019).

5.14.2 The President

Presidents have the power to develop and formulate policy on a vast array of issues. The level of personal attention that presidents give to the "nuts and bolts" process of developing a policy varies and reflects the executive's leadership style. For instance, President Bill Clinton preferred to create task forces and working groups comprising members of Congress, career civil servants, and his own staff. The Welfare Reform Act of 1996 was a joint effort between executive branch staff and state governors. Clinton's unsuccessful attempt at health care reform was developed by a task force directed by Hillary Clinton. In contrast, President George W. Bush preferred a more centralized style of decision making. Many of his policy initiatives were created by a small group of advisors who worked in the President's inner circle (Stewart Hedge & Lester, 2008).

5.14.3 Congress

Policy design and formulation is the primary responsibility of Congress. The legislative branch both develops new legislation and provides oversight and legislative review of existing legislation. House members passed House Resolution 1, the *For the People Act*, early in the 116th Congress. The legislation would address current issues in voting, campaign spending, redistricting, and public ethics. The *For the People Act* was created by a coalition of House members and was inspired by constituents who called for these reforms (Overby, 2019).

5.14.4 Interest Groups

Pluralism, introduced in chapter 4, posits that policy is shaped by bargaining, negotiation, and compromise among various actors in the policy process. Interest groups are one of the most prolific actors in the pluralist model. They animate the design and formulation phases and are, on occasion, directly involved in the actual writing of policy. Of course, this level of involvement can be positive or negative. Like bureaucrats, interest groups often have a deeper understanding of technical issues than do elected politicians. Conversely, interest groups possess extreme power to influence policy. Interest groups can "structure policy outcomes in a way that is characterized by corruption, backroom politics, a lack of long-range planning, and injustice" (Stewart Hedge Lester, 2008).

5.14.5 Think Tanks

Think tanks are policy planning organizations that conduct research and advocate for a vast array of topics, from social issues to economic policy, military, and cultural issues. Most think tanks are nonprofit organizations, but some are funded by the government, interest groups, or even corporations. Think tanks employ leading scholars and prominent political figures who review current academic research on topics of interest. They develop recommendations for policies and programs that they believe will solve pressing public problems. The recommendations are sent to the President, Congress, and the media (Dye, 2013). The Brookings Institute, the Heritage Foundation, and the CATO Institute are all prominent fixtures among the Washington elite. The influence of such think tanks should not be underestimated. When the time came for President Trump to nominate a Supreme Court Justice to replace Antonin Scalia, he relied on the Heritage Foundation to develop a list of potential justices (Mahler, 2018).

5.15 CASE STUDY: DESIGN AND FORMULATION OF THE ACA

Early in the policy design process, President Obama discussed a *causal* link between the goals of the new health care legislation and "skyrocketing health care costs." He argued that by lowering the two most expensive healthcare costs, emergency room visits and chronic illnesses, healthcare costs would decrease overall. Accomplishing this goal would mean changing the rules of the healthcare system. People could no longer be uninsured, insurance companies could not exclude patients with preexisting conditions, and insurance companies must provide preventative care measures to encourage people to go to a primary care doctor instead of using the more expensive emergency room. Thus, early in the policy design phase, the Obama administration created a causal link between the policy goal, lower health care costs, and the factors that they believed caused those costs.

When President Obama took office, he believed that both Congress and the American public would support sweeping health care changes. Despite early efforts to convince stakeholders, Obama realized that his ideas would not be met with open arms in Congress. This knowledge changed the policy design strategy considerably. Rather than taking a purely rational comprehensive approach to policy making, Obama recognized that he would have to make concessions if he wanted health care reform to pass. Those concessions might result in the elimination of some of the components that he originally wanted to include in the final policy. For example, Obama had planned to include a public option insurance plan that would compete directly with private insurance companies. The goal of this plan was to create more competition and reduce health care costs. Opponents resisted the public option, so it was never added to the bill. In the end, Obama decided that he wanted to pass health care reform more than he wanted to fight for the public option (Morris et al., 2019). In this instance, initial plans for policy design had to be modified to gain support from key policymakers.

The public option is not the only example of adjustments made to the policy design process. President Obama studied Bill Clinton's earlier and unsuccessful attempts at health care reform and resolved to include a coalition of key actors in the policy design process. Doctors, insurance companies, pharmaceutical representatives, labor unions, and elected officials all assembled to design a plan that suited the desires of a vast constituency. The coalition developed a set of shared principles that they would use to guide the new health care reform law. These goals included sharing responsibility for universal health coverage, improving affordability and quality, reducing waste and spending, while focusing on preventative care and community health (Morris et al., 2019). Policy designers knew that to get the policy to pass, they would need to take an *incremental* approach to health care reform. Instead of deconstructing the entire system, they maintained the current U.S. health care system (private insurance) and focused on incremental changes, such as employer-sponsored insurance, Medicare, and Medicaid. The coalition also made *equity* and *efficiency* two of the key pillars of the plan by focusing on affordability, accessibility, diversity, and inclusivity. Protection for individuals with preexisting conditions was a priority, along with prohibiting insurance companies from capping the amount of health care coverage that individuals could receive throughout their lifetime. In one speech, Obama remarked that we "should promote best practices, not the most expensive ones" (Stolberg, 2009).

Policymakers designed a health care policy that gave power to state governments to implement the policy as they saw fit. State officials could adapt the policy to meet conditions in their state, thus avoiding the "one size fits all" moniker. State autonomy was included in the bill because there was a sense that Republicans would support a health care plan with a decentralized implementation strategy. After all, state's rights continued to be a central tenant of the Republican Party, even after Ronald Reagan's presidency (Morris et al., 2019). In the initial policy design, all states were required to expand their Medicaid programs to everyone living below the federal poverty line. States that refused to expand Medicaid would be sanctioned and have their federal Medicaid funds withheld. The Supreme Court later ruled in *NFIB v. Sebelius* (2012) that this provision was unconstitutional. The federal government then decided to take a different approach and formulated the policy to include a system of rewards—more significant medical assistance funding—to states that chose to expand Medicaid. To further entice states to expand Medicaid, policymakers promised to pay 100% of each state's program costs during the first two years of the ACA's implementation.

In retrospect, it is remarkable that the ACA became law. The policy was passed in an extremely divisive political environment. The $900 billion price tag—combined with an economy recovering from a recession—was a sticking point for policymakers. The policy design coalition included a plan to pay for the ACA primarily through new taxes. This solution alone created additional opposition. The ACA faced numerous legal challenges and an uncertain future once President Trump was elected into office. The successful passage of the ACA is due in no small part to those who designed the policy. They knew that they would have to make concessions to gain the necessary support. They focused on providing equity and efficiency throughout the process, and when sanctions were unsuccessful, they created incentives for compliance.

5.16 CRITICAL THINKING QUESTIONS – POLICY FORMULATION AND THE ACA

- What decision making style best describes the way that the ACA was designed? Did the Obama administration take a rational or garbage can approach? In what ways does the ACA follow an incremental approach to policy making?
- What compromises were made to persuade Congress to pass the ACA? Do you feel that making concessions to "just get the bill passed" is a good way to govern?
- Explain how the policy goals of equity and efficiency were incorporated in the design process.

5.17 CHAPTER SUMMARY

In this chapter we discuss how policies are designed and formulated. The first step in policy design is to start with the goal. Deborah Stone (2002) argues that public policy goals incorporate four major concepts: equity, efficiency, security, and liberty. Policymakers also have a number of policy tools at their disposal. Inducements are options for changing people's behavior through rewards or punishments, sanctions, and incentives. Finally, policymakers must decide between potential solutions. We discuss three decision making models, the rational comprehensive model, incrementalism, and the garbage can model.

5.18 KEY TERMS

- Efficiency
- Garbage Can Model

- Impacts
- Incrementalism
- Inducements
- Inputs
- Outcomes
- Outputs
- Policy design
- Policy formulation
- Policy tools
- Rational Comprehensive Model
- Security

5.19 REFERENCES

Anderson, James. 1990. *Public Policymaking: An Introduction*. Boston, MA: Houghton Mifflin.

Blackmon, David. 2019. "Florida Fracking Ban Bill as a Classic Government Solution in Search of a Problem." *Forbes*, November 6, 2019. https://www.forbes.com/sites/davidblackmon/2019/11/06/florida-fracking-ban-bill-is-a-classic-government-solution-in-search-of-a-problem/#45029e25635e.

Birkland, Thomas. 2019. *An Introduction to the Policy Process: Theories, Concepts, and Models of Public Policy Making*. New York, NY: Routledge.

Carnevale, Anthony, Tamara Jayasundera, and Artem Gulish. 2016. *Divided Recovery: College Haves and Have-Nots*. Georgetown University: Center on Education and the Workforce. https://cew.georgetown.edu/wp-content/uploads/Americas-Divided-Recovery-web.pdf

Cohen, Michael, James March, and Johan Olsen. 1972. A Garbage Can Model of Organizational Choice. *Administrative Science Quarterly*. 17: 1-25.

Dodaro, Gene. 2019. *The Nation's Fiscal Health: Actions Needed to Achieve Long-Term Fiscal Sustainability*. GAO-19-611T. Washington, DC. Accessed November 15, 2019. https://www.gao.gov/assets/700/699992.pdf

Funnell, S. and Rogers, P. 2011. *Purposeful Program Theory: Effective Use of Theories of Change and Logic Models*. San Francisco, CA: John Wiley & Sons.

Government Accountability Office. 2019. *Additional Opportunities Reduce Fragmentation, Overlap, and Duplication and Achieve Billions in Financial Benefits*. GAO-19-285. Washington, DC. Accessed November 15, 2019 https://www.gao.gov/products/GAO-19-285SP

Hembree, Diana. 2018. "New Report Finds Student Debt Burden Has Disastrous Domino Effect on Millions of Americans." *Forbes*, Nov 1 2018. https://www.forbes.com /

sites/dianahembree/2018/11/01/new-report-finds-student-debt-burden-has-disastrous-domino-effect-on-millions-of-americans/#1d60c9f812d1

Hobbes, Thomas. 1968. *1588-1679. Leviathan.* Baltimore, MD: Penguin Books.

Howlett, Michael. 2010. *Designing Public Policy: Principles and Instruments*, London: Routledge.

Insurance Institute for Highway Safety. n.d. "Speed." Accessed November 15, 2019. https://www.iihs.org/topics/speed#effects-of-speed-limits-on-safety

Lindblom, Charles. 1959. "The Science of 'Muddling Through," *Public Administration Review*. 19: 79–88.

Mahler, Jonathan. 2018. "How One Conservative Think Tank is Stocking Trump's Government." *New York Times*, June 20, 2018. https://www.nytimes.com/2018/06/20/ magazine/trump-government-heritage-foundation-think-tank.html June 20 2018

Morris, John, Martin Mayer, Robert Kenter, and Luisa Lucero. 2020. *State Politics and the Affordable Care Act: Choices and Decisions.* New York, NY: Taylor & Francis.

Nagourney, Adam, and David Sanger. 2018. "Hawaii Panics After Alert About Incoming Missile is Sent in Error." *New York Times*, January 13, 2018. https://www.nytimes.com/2018/01 /13/us/hawaii-missile.html

Overby, Peter. 2019. "House Democrats Introduce Anti-Corruption Bill as Symbolic First Act." *NPR*, January 5, 2019. https://www.npr.org/2019/01/05/682286587/house-democrats-introduce-anti-corruption-bill-as-symbolic-first-act

Schneider, Anne, and Helen Ingram. 1997. *Policy Design for Democracy.* Lawrence, KS: University Press of Kansas.

Simon, Herbert. 1947. *Administrative Behavior: A Study of Decision-Making Processes in Administrative Organization* (1st ed.) New York, NY: Macmillan.

Simon, Herbert. 1956. "Rational Choice and the Structure of the Environment," *Psychological Review*, 63(2): 129-138.

Stone, Deborah. 1997. *Policy Paradox: The Art of Political Decision Making.* New York, NY: W.W. Norton.

Tieghi, Alexandra. 2017. "Fundamentals Unpacked: Outcomes and Outputs in the Public Sector." *Centre for Public Impact* (blog). October 4, 2017. Accessed November 1, 2019. https://www.centreforpublicimpact.org/outcomes-and-outputs-public-sector/

Worth, Michael J. 2016. *Nonprofit Management: Principles and Practice.* Fourth Edition ed. Los Angeles: SAGE Publications.

Yale University Library Online Exhibit. n.d. "Selling Smoke: Tobacco Advertising and Anti-Smoking Campaigns." Accessed November 15, 2019 http://exhibits.library.yale.edu /exhibits/show/sellingsmoke

6 Policy Implementation

6.1 CHAPTER OBJECTIVES:

- Outline the major steps in the implementation process.
- Discuss the government actors responsible for implementing policy.
- Explain the factors affecting successful policy implementation.
- Compare the procedures policymakers utilize to overcome obstacles.

Casual observers may think the policy process is complete once a law is passed or an executive order is issued. However, the policy, once authorized, must be implemented. **Implementation** is the "set of activities directed toward putting a program into effect" (Jones, 1984). Implementation is a complex process and can take months, or even years, to fully complete. Kraft and Furlong (2018) consider three activities crucial to successful implementation: organization, interpretation, and application. Organization refers to the administration of the program, particularly the resources allocated, and the personnel assigned. Interpretation addresses how the policy is understood by those responsible for administering the policy. Lastly, application is how the policy objectives are carried out.

Executives—presidents, governors, and mayors—are generally responsible for executing policy by way of bureaucratic agencies. Examples of such agencies include the Department of Health and Human Services at the federal level, the Department of Transportation at the state level, and the Parks and Recreation Department at the local level. Executives are also responsible for selecting agency heads to oversee policy execution. Presidents generally have appointed officials who agree with them on program objectives (commonly referred to as "yes-men") and are experts in the field; they may also receive their appointment as patronage for supporting the executive in their bid for elected office. William Barr, whom President Trump appointed to replace Attorney General Sessions, was a proponent of uncontested executive power and is considered a yes-man by many. Conversely, George Romney as Secretary of the Department of Housing and Urban Development and Clifford Hardin as Secretary of the Department of Agriculture were chosen by President Nixon not as spokesmen for his agenda but as spokesmen of the interests they served (Nathan, 1975).

Though the executive is responsible for policy execution, agencies rely on funding to administer programs. The executive and legislative branch each put forth their budget priorities and must negotiate to reach a final agreement before a budget is passed. The budget will allocate funds through appropriations. Agencies, therefore, are constrained by both the legislature and the executive, particularly during periods of divided government. Therefore, it is incumbent on agency heads to maintain a strong, positive relationship with both executive and legislative branches. The appropriation of policy does not guarantee its success. The policy relies on personnel, funding, and buy-in by bureaucrats to implement legislation as directed. Furthermore, policies may be overridden when a new executive is elected and the composition of the legislature changes—when, for example, party control in Congress or the state legislature shifts—which could affect appropriations. Overrides can also occur if bureaucrats change their opinion on the policy, either due to personnel turnover or changes in resource allocation.

Implementation is an ongoing endeavor that will continue until the policy is terminated. Policy administrators, particularly the managers, must continuously monitor the policy and protect it from those who would like to see it fail. Bardach (1977) contends that policy implementation can be looked at as one views a machine. A machine, much like public policy, is complex and has many moving parts that must work together to produce the desired output. This chapter will explore the implementation process by considering who implements policy, what factors influence implementation, which action levers policy makers can utilize in the process, and the ways scholars approach the study of implementation.

> **Stop and Think**
>
> Think of a time when you were responsible for carrying out a task. Who proposed the task? Who was responsible for overseeing the task's completion?

6.2 WHO IMPLEMENTS POLICY?

According to Weimer and Vining (2017), the implementation process involves **managers**, **doers**, and **fixers**. Managers assemble the policy machine and direct doers on how to implement the policy. They include senior supervisors and mid-level bureaucrats. Managers are directed by agency officials—like cabinet officials—to carry out policy and oversee the work of doers in the implementation process. It is important that managers favor the policy, or they may not be willing to expend personal or organizational resources to effectively implement the policy. Furthermore, when policy is ambiguous, managers who do not favor the policy may apply an interpretation that does not align with the intent of the policy maker.

Assuming the manager favors the policy and is capable of working with other managers when required, that manager must have the capacity to incentivize the doers. This capacity relies on various resources, most notably "authority, political support, and treasure" (Weimer and Vining, 2017). Managers must be able to assemble a policy machine with enough structure that the policy can be successfully implemented but remain flexible enough to adapt to change. Managers are also responsible for coordinating with other agencies if the policy requires **horizontal coordination**, whereby the policy relies on a number of agencies across one level of government to successfully execute the program. For example, President Obama issued the executive branch memorandum Deferred Action for Childhood Arrivals (DACA) on June 15, 2012. DACA required the coordination of the Department of Homeland Security, which oversaw the implementation; U.S. Immigration and Customs Enforcement (ICE); U.S. Citizenship and Immigration Services (USCIS); and U.S. Customs and Border Protection (CBP). For its successful implementation, DACA required not only buy-in from subordinate bureaucrats but also the successful coordination of agency leaders.

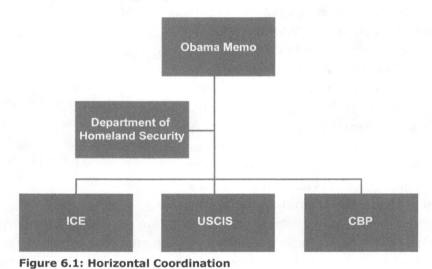

Figure 6.1: Horizontal Coordination
Source: Original Work
Attribution: Keith Lee
Source: CC BY-SA 4.0

6.2.1 Doers

Doers, on the other hand, often deal directly with clients at the street level and are called **street-level bureaucrats**. Street-level bureaucrats are directly responsible for service delivery and are those of whom most people think when they think of the bureaucracy. One major complaint many have with bureaucracy is unnecessary and burdensome red tape. The red tape is often seen at the street-level. Teachers and police officers commonly exemplify street-level bureaucrats; other examples include case workers, public defenders, and health department employees. Generally speaking, anyone responsible for delivering public services directly to the public is a street-level bureaucrat. According to Lipsky (1980), street-level bureaucrats are at the heart of political debate involving service delivery for two primary reasons: (1) "debates over proper scope and focus of governmental services are essentially debates over the scope and function of these public employees," and (2) "street-level bureaucrats have considerable impact over people's lives." Furthermore, they "determine eligibility" and "oversee the treatment citizens receive."

In order to effectively implement policy, doers rely on resources provided by managers, including staff, time, and money. These resources can be used to incentivize doers who do not favor a specific policy and so do not want to comply. Much like managers, doers can hinder policy implementation in a variety of ways, most notably through tokenism, massive resistance, and social entropy (Bardach, 1977). Tokenism occurs when implementation appears to be going as planned publicly, while behind the scenes doers are only pushing a small, or "token," contribution. An example of this type of situation would be a policy requiring agencies to hire more women in certain departments to ensure even representation in the agency. However, rather than completing the requirement as defined, the agency may simply promote a woman or a number of women to higher ranks to create the appearance of equality in the agency. Tokenism can also be seen when doers delay compliance or provide inferior service. Tokenism in practice allows opponents of the policy an opening to point out the poor implementation, which could lead to policy overhaul or termination. Doers engage in massive resistance when they withhold specific program elements until administrators sanction their behavior. However, if agency heads, fixers, and/or managers are unable to quell the resistance fast enough, the policy could fail, particularly if there is political opposition, competing policy alternatives, or lack of constituent support. In essence, tokenism can be resolved with carrots, or incentives, whereas massive resistance relies on sticks, or sanctions.

According to Bardach (1977), social entropy manifests itself in three distinct problems: incompetence, variability, and coordination. Incompetence involves the inability of perfectly compliant doers to successfully implement policy, even when policy directives are clear. Organizational turnover is a primary contributor to incompetent bureaucrats, as they are unable to develop the skills necessary for successful policy implementation. This concept rings true particularly among street-level bureaucrats who are new to their positions and who may not be familiar with organizational norms or policies. Furthermore, bureaucrats at all levels may lack an understanding of the vast number of policies the organization is responsible for carrying out. All of these factors cripple well-timed policy execution.

Variability, on the other hand, stems from a systematic approach to policy-making that is not equipped to handle various societal issues that affect parties responsible for executing the policy. This is particularly true when **vertical coordination** is required. Vertical coordination, unlike horizontal coordination, does not rely on agencies or other units across a single level to work together for policy implementation. Rather, the policy calls for top-down coordination whereby a senior official works with subordinate organizations, individuals, or agencies to implement a policy. Furthermore, the top-down approach can consist of more than two levels of government. For example, the No Child Left Behind Act of 2001 (NCLB) relied on vertical coordination at more than two levels. The act required states to develop standards that could be assessed and that would demonstrate improved education outcomes for individual students in order to receive federal funding. States were then responsible for holding individual school districts accountable for performing assessments and demonstrating Adequate Yearly Progress (AYP) by meeting "high standards." High standards, in this case, is an ambiguous term that was left up to the states to define. Critics of the policy argued that the law reduced teacher freedom in the classroom and required educators to teach to the test. Furthermore, critics argued that states and school districts lacked adequate control to alter their curriculum and standards based on community needs. At its core, NCLB relied on doers—for example, school board officials and teachers—to pursue high standards and quality assessment. The criticism from parents, teachers, and officials required the policy machine to be overhauled to better deliver a policy that would in turn provide better educational outcomes. President Obama granted exemptions to 32 states in 2012, and the law was replaced in 2015 by the Every Student Succeeds Act, which reduced the federal government's role by allowing more flexibility within states.

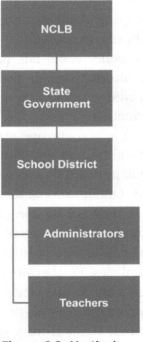

Figure 6.2: Vertical Coordination
Source: Original Work
Attribution: Keith Lee
License: CC BY-SA 4.0

Finally, coordination problems arise when individuals responsible for carrying out the policy within different organizations interpret the policy differently or vary in their level of support for the policy. The term generally refers to horizontal coordination, mentioned above, regarding the role of managers to work well with others, but could also refer to vertical coordination. For the sake of simplicity, we will only consider horizontal coordination which requires parallel cooperation, since vertical coordination relies on a manager-subordinate relationship that can force cooperation. Conversely, horizontal coordination relies on mutually accepted goals that are deemed efficient and cost effective. The process requires agency heads, managers, and doers to agree on an outcome favorable to all parties. Furthermore, doers are those most burdened by coordination requirements. Policy makers may provide resources at different levels to coordinating agencies, which could result in one or more agencies lacking the necessary resources to perform their duties effectively. In sum, poor coordination among agencies, particularly among doers, may result in tokenism or massive resistance. In these cases, fixers may be asked to step in to rectify coordination problems to ensure policy success.

> **Stop and Think**
>
> Have you ever had to carry out a task that required you to work with another group? How does it compare to coordinating within an organization? Under what conditions might it be harder to work within a single organization?

6.2.2 Fixers

As noted by Rhodes (2016), the shift in public administration to the New Public Governance (NPG) model calls on public servants to become agents who manage "complex, non-routing issues, policies, and relationships." Fixers exemplify this call as they are the individuals called up to work within the policy arena to alleviate tension between managers and doers or to alleviate tensions that develop when coordination problems arise. Fixers can be directly involved with policy creation, as can, for example, a legislative staff member, or on the ground level supporting a policy and ensuring its successful implementation, as can a manager or doer who favors the policy and needs agency coordination for policy implementation. The former will likely work between managers and doers to determine what resources are needed for successful implementation, whereas the latter will serve as the eyes and ears for managers to assist in getting non-compliant or reluctant doers in line. Fixers may also be required to work with policy makers, at the recommendation of managers and doers, to add a new policy dimension for successful implementation.

Fixers, to be successful, must be capable of anticipating problems before they develop. As we will discuss in the next section, fixers are better suited for developing contingency plans based on **alternative scenario planning**. Additionally, fixers must be coalition builders, particularly when working with multiple agencies. Majority coalition building requires the fixer to find common ground among the most receptive agencies in order to get the least receptive agencies on board. Lastly, fixers need to be familiar with the various factors that hinder policy implementation and work with policy makers in addressing those factors.

6.3 FACTORS INFLUENCING POLICY IMPLEMENTATION

Beyond the relationships and characteristics of the actors implementing policy, several factors contribute to the implementation process. Brewer and deLeon (1983) list six such factors: (1) source of the policy, (2) clarity of the policy, (3) support for the policy, (4) complexity of administration, (5) incentives for implementers, and (6) resource allocation.

The policy source refers to the party or parties responsible for creating a policy. In American politics, this means one of the branches of government. The remainder of this section will frame each factor in relation to the federal government, but the subnational counterparts can easily be substituted, for example, by considering a state's governor or a town's mayor when the president or executive branch is named. Presidents establish policy primarily through executive orders, proclamations, and memos. President Trump issued Executive Order 13793 on April 27, 2017 which called for accountability and whistleblower protection at the Department of Veterans Affairs. The policy created the Office of Accountability and Whistleblower Protection and a special assistant to serve as the director of the office. Congress establishes policy through legislation, such as the Patient Protection and Affordable Care Act in 2010. Lastly, the courts can establish policy by ruling on issues that affect the public at large, that is, issues pertaining to civil rights, voting rights, and education.

The policy source influences implementation due to the nature of policy administration, which is controlled by both the president and Congress. The president, through the bureaucracy, exercises great leverage over which policy is implemented and which policy, or portion of a policy, is ignored. Nevertheless, Congress possesses several constitutional tools, most notably appropriations and oversight. Taken together, the bureaucracy can serve as a pawn

Stop and Think

Think back to the task above that you were asked to accomplish. What factors led to successful completion? What obstacles did you face? What lessons did you learn that may improve your ability to complete future objectives?

in a policy battle between the president and Congress, which can hinder implementation. This is further complicated by the remaining five factors.

The next factor, clarity of the policy, concerns the precision of the policy intent. For example, the executive order mentioned above grants the Secretary of Veterans Affairs great discretion in how the policy is carried out, which will depend on their support for the policy. On the other hand, some policy directives are explicit in their intent, such as the desegregation of public schools, but their implementation is inconsistently carried out due to ambiguities on how they should be executed. The *Brown v. Board of Education* (1954) decision, which ruled that segregation was unlawful but did not explicitly state how to integrate schools, is one example of this phenomena. In fact, the parties were ordered to reappear before the court the following year to discuss how public schools were to be integrated. The court ruled it should happen with "all deliberate speed." In this case, the intent was clear, but implementation was ambiguous. Ambiguity like this results in implementers gaining significant authority in how the policy is carried out.

Third, support for the policy will dictate its success. The policy relies on support from not only the people but also the authorities overseeing policy execution and implementation, a support that is absolutely necessary. The president can issue an executive order, such as EO 13793 mentioned above, but Congress must appropriate the funds necessary to establish the new office and appoint the executive director. This condition is explicitly stated in Section 2 of the order: "The VA shall provide funding and administrative support for the Office, consistent with applicable law and *subject to the availability of appropriations*" (emphasis added).

The fourth factor is the complexity of the administrative requirements for implementation. The implementation of the policy can deviate from the policy maker's intention if the administration of the policy requires horizontal and/ or vertical coordination. Horizontal coordination is relevant when agencies or organizations operate in tandem to ensure a policy is executed as designed. Vertical coordination is necessary when a policy passes through one agency or organization to another before it is fully implemented. Complex policies often rely on both horizontal and vertical coordination, which can result in policy implementation that does not match the original intent, particularly when agencies are expected to share revenue to execute the policy. Revenue sharing results in agency competition for resources which, in turn, affects individual behavior, either positively, for example, in agencies that secure the necessary funding, or negatively, such as with agencies that feel shortchanged in the sharing process. Funding, as noted above, provides an incentive for successful implementation by managers and doers.

The fifth factor that affects policy implementation involves incentives for administrators. Incentives can be broken down into three modes (Brewer and deLeon, 1983): replicating the economic marketplace to achieve efficiency, organizational restructuring, and bureaucratic competition. The economic marketplace appears in the hiring of private contractors to carry out public service, such as trash pickup at the local level or private contractors assisting with national defense as with Lockheed Martin which manufactures weapons. However, agency officials and managers may oppose private contracting if the money appropriated for the contracting comes directly from their budget—unless, of course, their budget is increased to reflect the additional cost. Organizational restructuring may also have a negative impact on public policy implementation. Policy makers may propose restructuring to improve the chances of implementation, but doing so may affect service delivery for an established policy. Therefore, agency employees may be reluctant to deliver on the new policy if they favor established policies. Furthermore, behavior studies indicate people are change averse and prefer the status quo. Lastly, bureaucratic competition provides greater opportunity for success. Theobald and Nicholson-Crotty (2005) provide an example from the 1960s. The policy issue at the time concerned drugs and addiction, and two agencies competed for resources to solve the problem: the National Institute of Mental Health (NIMH) and the Federal Bureau of Narcotics (FBN). The NIMH argued that addiction should be treated as a disease, whereas the FBN proposed a law enforcement solution. No matter which agency won the battle, policy makers would ultimately achieve their goal of addressing drug use and addiction.

Lastly, resource allocation greatly influences the implementation of public policy. The example used earlier ordered the new office within Veterans Affairs to be established within forty-five days. However, as noted above, successful implementation hinged on adequate appropriations, which rely on Congress to act if the president's executive order is to be dutifully executed. Another example would be a policy change that affected clients at the street-level, but agencies were not given the resources to train employees or hire specialized staff to oversee the execution. This issue could result in poor implementation due to tokenism and massive resistance by the doers responsible for carrying out the policy.

Taken together, the factors listed above highlight additional complexities in the policy process during implementation. Furthermore, these factors provide a deeper understanding of the relationship between policy makers, the source, managers, and doers. However, as the next section outlines, policy makers have at their disposal a number of "action levers" by which to influence implementation (Starling, 1988).

6.4 ACTION LEVERS

The factors discussed above highlight the challenges policy makers may face when their policy is implemented. However, Starling (1988) provides a broad overview of four "action levers" that can be used during the policy design phase to encourage successful implementation. "**Design levers**" are mechanisms used during the formulation phase. "**Operating system levers**" are guidelines put in place to guide the policy from design to implementation. "**Organizational levers**" pertain to how an agency responsible for policy implementation is established or restructured. Lastly, "**political levers**" refer to the actions taken by policy makers and policy supporters to quell dissension among opponents, such as interest groups and political opposition. This section will discuss the first two, since organizational and political levers, although not necessarily defined as "levers," are considered in earlier chapters.

6.4.1 Design Levers

Two design levers are considered here: proposal imprecision and organizational simplification. Contrary to Brewer and deLeon, Starling (1988) contends that lack of clarity or precision can help a policy maker. Precise goals can centralize organizations, particularly those relied upon to implement the policy, and they may begin to consider ways to obstruct implementation if they fear favorable alternatives will not be considered. This is particularly problematic when dealing with policy that does not have much political or constituent support. Furthermore, issues that are explicitly stated will attract opposition that will likely unite around a single aspect of the proposed policy—as with, for example, the individual mandate in the Affordable Care Act—to better their chances of defeating the policy. Additionally, sponsors may have a difficult time walking back a precise policy proposal in the face of backlash, public or otherwise, considering such a move would signal to the opposition that the policy as proposed is flawed, thereby providing naysayers with more ammunition when attacking the proposal.

Starling (1984) further contends that "policies should be designed to minimize the amount of human behavior that needs to be changed." Unfortunately, this advice is challenging, given the complexity of public policy, especially considering the ever-growing administrative state. Furthermore, policy originating within the legislature is likely to include multiple agencies and agenda items, given the nature of Congress and the prevalence of logrolling.

6.4.2 Operating System Levers

Starling (1998) considers four actions that officials can use to assist with implementation: start-up decisions, public relations decisions, incentive decisions, and contingency decisions. The start-up period is the time from policy authorization to full implementation, or what Starling refers to as the "steady state period." The length of the start-up period depends on the specific policy. For example, changing the structure of the Office of Veterans Affairs could be considered urgent, given the nature of veteran care in the U.S., and thus warrant immediate implementation. Furthermore, the changes authorized were relatively straightforward and could be implemented easily as long as funding was provided. Less urgent policies, such as the Affordable Care Act, could be implemented incrementally to allow time for ironing out issues that arose during the start-up period.

Starling further considers learning curves and scheduling. Learning curves are a way of thinking about agency efficiency over time. Agencies that do not undergo significant changes, such as high turnover rates or changes in leadership, can utilize lessons learned from past policy implementation to develop more efficient practices. Similarly, scheduling plays an integral role in implementation during the start-up period and can be more effective in agencies that have a clear understanding of time to policy implementation. Furthermore, agencies can consider the expected time to reach the steady state period to improve their chances of policy success. Two factors worth considering are the budget cycle and the election cycle. Policy authorization is the first step in the policy process, but policies cannot be implemented without sufficient funding. Therefore, policy authorization immediately prior to the legislature submitting their appropriation may improve the policies' survival. Authorization given with a long waiting period before appropriations will allow political opponents an opportunity to lobby against the policy in an attempt to kill it. Similarly, policy makers must consider the election cycle. Politically popular proposals may benefit from implementation immediately before an election to give officials an opportunity to use the policy in campaign material, whereas a policy that may affect an elected official's reelection prospects is best suited for implementation immediately after an election. For example, a majority of Americans in 2010 supported the repeal of "Don't Ask, Don't Tell," a policy implemented under President Bill Clinton, but individual members of Congress would not risk political capital to support the repeal. However, Congress did support the repeal during the lame duck period immediately after the 2010 midterm elections.

Policy success also depends on public relations decisions, especially in our current age of social media and twenty-four hour news coverage. Policy makers and those responsible for implementing the policy must communicate with a wide variety of individuals, organizations, and interest groups. To do so effectively, particularly in an era of hyper partisanship, policy makers rely on elected officials and agency heads to be consistent when using talking points outlining the policy proposal. Examples of partisan policy include the Affordable Care Act, immigration reform, and changes to such social programs as Medicaid, Medicare, and Social Security. Policy makers and agency heads regularly appear on various news programs throughout the week, and particularly Sunday morning broadcasts, commenting on controversial policy proposals.

Similarly, social media use as a public relations tool has become widespread. Policy makers can use social media to advocate for policy, while the political opposition will use the platforms to condemn it. Social media allows various mediums to be used to drive public opinion and make the public aware: emotive videos on YouTube, live streams on Facebook, polls on Twitter, and memes on Instagram are all examples of platforms used to inform and manipulate the people's views on policy.

Starling (1988) noted media is generally adversarial and anti-agency. Furthermore, he argued:

> Exposé titillates readers more than praise. In an agency with sound public relations, this {adversarial} bias is countered with cooperation, thoughtfulness, and professionalism. Officials answer questions from the media promptly. When executives cannot answer questions for the media promptly, they make every effort to be helpful, supplying the reporter with story material whenever possible...every effort is made not to mislead reporters, even by what is left unsaid.

It is safe to say that this assumption is no longer accurate. Policy makers are quick to stick to their talking points, often ignoring challenging questions and redirecting the conversation to their views on the issue. Furthermore, the bias is no longer countered with "cooperation, thoughtfulness, and professionalism" but by policy makers and their surrogates calling out the media for their bias. Similarly, the twenty-four hour news cycle demands commentary rather than strict reporting, that is, discussing the fact and allowing viewers or readers to draw conclusions, which shapes public views on the policy. It is no secret that news outlets, in most cases, now cater to one political party and/or ideology instead of remaining unbiased.

Beyond the media, policy makers must convince other government officials and interest groups that the policy is worth pursuing. Achieving this feat relies on a different form of public relations based on strong personal relationships. Agency officials who favor the policy, unlike advocates and opponents in elected office, must build positive relationships and court those who are undecided and in a position to push the policy through the policy making process. However, as noted above, highly partisan policies may be unaffected by these relationships. Therefore, policy makers need to have contingency plans in place if the intended policy does not appear possible.

> **Stop and Think**
>
> Find an example online of a time when a policy maker was criticized by the media and did not respond with "cooperation, thoughtfulness, and professionalism." Next, try to find an article that does respond in a manner outlined above. Which one was easier to find? Why might this be the case?

Contingency decisions require policy analysts to consider not only competing alternatives but also alternatives that closely resemble the policy initially proposed. Policy alternatives may include scaled back versions of the initial policy that may not achieve the desired result but nevertheless address shortcomings in the proposed policy. Beyond listing and considering policy alternatives, analysts can also conduct alternative scenario planning, whereby they consider future events that may result in policy failure, particularly during the start-up period. Starling suggests using four scenarios: two that are "bleak," one that is average (or expected), and one that is "bright" (Starling, 1988).

Lastly, policy makers must consider incentive decisions to get bureaucrats to change their behavior. Policy makers can use cost-benefit analysis to determine incentives necessary for policy success. Luft (1976) contends cost-benefit analysis does not require an evaluation of monetary terms, which may be useful when considering contingency decisions, but should look at non-monetary terms instead, such as resistance to change by individuals.

Taken together, the four operating levers work in tandem to achieve policy success. A long start-up period may be useful for policy that is not urgent but may allow more time for the opposition to undermine public relations efforts by policy advocates. Therefore, it is incumbent on policy makers to consider contingency plans when policy failure is imminent, as well as select the right incentives to gain support from policy implementers. The success of these decisions is largely influenced by the organizational structure in which the policy is being considered and the methods used to implement the policy.

6.5 APPROACHES TO SUCCESSFUL IMPLEMENTATION

The two primary methods for achieving successful implementation of a policy are the **top-down approach** and the **bottom-up approach**. Both approaches have strengths and weaknesses and should be applied on a case-by-case basis. However, more recent scholarship has proposed a **third-generation approach** which we will discuss in the following section.

The top-down approach uses forward mapping and moves policy from the top, that is, from policy makers to implementation. The process requires policy makers to make predictions about the survival and success of the policy at various stages. As mentioned before, policy making is a complex process that often includes horizontal and vertical coordination. A policy maker using the top-down approach will try to predict the outcomes at each level to include the interactions between agencies and organizations. The bottom-up approach, on the other hand, utilizes backward mapping which focuses on the behavior the policy maker wishes to change at the street-level and works from the bottom to achieve that change.

As stated above, top-down and bottom-up approaches are not without weaknesses. The top-down approach relies on clear and precise objectives, which can be problematic for reasons stated earlier. Furthermore, the top-down approach relies on policy makers and analysts to predict mid-level and street-level bureaucratic behavior, which is not an exact science and is further complicated when considering vertical and horizontal coordination issues. Similarly, the bottom-up approach cannot fully predict human behavior, particularly that of street-level bureaucrats. However, street-level bureaucrats can be motivated through various incentives, such as funding for policy implementation or repercussions for noncompliance, so achieving the policy outcomes is just a matter of correctly predicting the level and type of coercion necessary.

Even considering their weaknesses, both approaches can still be useful in specific situations. The top-down model is best suited for single policy issues with little coordination, while bottom-up methods are better when the policy is broad and multiple agencies utilize street-level bureaucrats to implement the policy. Nevertheless, Richard Elmore (1985, cited in Birkland, 2019) combined the two approaches. Goggin et al. (1990, cited in Birkland, 2019) further extended the work started by Elmore to develop a theory on the premise that "implementation is as much a matter of negotiation and communication as it is a matter of command," providing two additional propositions (Birkland, 2019):

- Clear messages sent by credible officials that are received by open-minded implementers, who have or are given sufficient resources, and can enact policies supported by affected groups create implementation success.

- Strategic delay on the part of states, while delaying the implementation of policies, can actually lead to improved implementation of policies through innovation, policy learning, bargaining, and the like.

In sum, these propositions indicate that implementation success relies on the following factors: clear and credible messages sent by the policy maker, sufficient resources provided to implementers, and a willingness to negotiate by all parties. In other words, policy making, especially implementation, is a complex process that deserves careful consideration by the analyst. As such, analysts should not treat every issue as a nail and a single technique as a hammer. Instead, they should diversify their toolbox to ensure the analysis is performed in a manner that increases the chance of policy success.

6.6 CASE STUDY: IMPLEMENTING THE AFFORDABLE CARE ACT

As outlined above, six factors affect policy implementation and three groups are responsible for implementing it. The first factor, source of policy, played a major role in the implementation of Obamacare. The partisan backdrop that grips the country under President Trump is nothing new and existed during President Obama's eight years in office. Policy proposals by Democrats were met with staunch opposition. Regarding the Obama agenda, then Speaker of the House John Boehner said, "We're going to do everything—and I mean everything we can do—to kill it, stop it, slow it down, whatever we can" (Barr, 2010). Likewise, Senate Minority Leader Mitch McConnell is quoted by the National Journal saying, "The single most important thing we want to achieve is for President Obama to be a one-term president" (Barr, 2010). The second factor, clarity of policy, was a major issue due to misinformation campaigns from the right and the Democrat's inability to deliver their message in a meaningful way. Speaker Pelosi, in an interview with Sarah Kliff (2017), expressed her one regret regarding the law: other Democrats not stepping up to defend the law, thus leading to "a sea of misinformation about her signature legislative achievement." One misinformation campaign was led by Americans for Prosperity, a conservative advocacy group. They began running campaigns in 2013 to cast doubt on the law (Peters, 2013). The messaging battle created confusion regarding the policy, which may have had a detrimental impact when it comes to political support, which leads us to the third, and arguably most important, factor: support for the policy.

In the case of Obamacare, the federal government is responsible for overseeing implementation (the manager). The ACA relied on both federal and state governments to successfully implement the law. The bill involved all 50 state governors, insurance commissioners, and Medicaid directors (the doers). The continued debate over Obamacare from its inception has been mired by partisan politics. Further complicating the implementation process was public support for the policy. More respondents, on average, have expressed disapproval of the law from its passage until a drastic shift after President Trump took office (Kirzinger, Muñana, and Brodie, 2019).

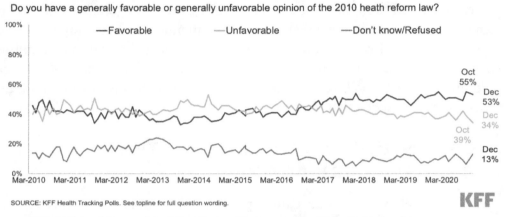

Figure 6.3: Larger Share of Public View ACA Favorably than Unfavorably
Source: Kaiser Family Foundation
Attribution: Kaiser Family Foundation
License: CC BY-NC-ND 4.0

Beyond public support, successful implementation also relies on the support of those implementing the policy. Even though the Democrats had control of the White House, and thus a great influence on bureaucratic behavior, implementation relied heavily on state support. Much like public support, state support was drawn on partisan lines. The ACA contained provisions that were left up to the states, including establishing insurance exchanges and expanding Medicaid. Only thirteen states have created state-based marketplaces, six have state-based marketplaces using the federal platform, and the remaining states rely on the federally facilitated marketplace (KFF, n.d.). State-based marketplaces perform all functions for the individual market, and consumers apply for coverage on websites maintained by each state. The federally facilitated marketplace, on the other hand, relies on HHS to perform all functions, and consumers apply for coverage via the federal Healthcare.gov site. The middle ground, state-based marketplaces using the federal platform, functions the same as state-based marketplaces, but consumers use Healthcare.gov to enroll in coverage.

The major provision contested by states is Medicaid expansion. The law mandated expansion, but the mandate was challenged in *National Federation of Independent Business v. Sebelius* (2012). The ruling declared the mandate unconstitutional by violating the 10th Amendment, thus leaving governors to decide whether their state would expand Medicaid. As of 2019, fourteen states have opted out of expansion. However, it is worth noting some states, including Georgia and Kansas, are considering expansion while others, including Missouri and Wyoming, have plans to place their expansion decisions on a future ballot (KFF, 2019).

State	Party Control	Exchange Type*	Medicaid Expansion?
Alabama	Republican	FFM	No
Alaska	Republican	FFM	Yes
Arizona	Republican	FFM	Yes
Arkansas	Republican	SBM-FP	Yes
California	Democrat	SBM	Yes
Colorado	Democrat	SBM	Yes
Connecticut	Democrat	SBM	Yes
Delaware	Democrat	FCM	Yes
District of Columbia	-	SBM	Yes
Florida	Republican	FCM	No
Georgia	Republican	FCM	No
Hawaii	Democrat	FCM	Yes
Idaho	Republican	SBM	Yes
Illinois	Democrat	FFM	Yes
Indiana	Republican	FFM	Yes
Iowa	Republican	FFM	Yes
Kansas	Democrat	FFM	No
Kentucky	Republican	SBM-FP	Yes
Louisiana	Democrat	FFM	Yes
Maine	Democrat	FFM	Yes
Maryland	Republican	SBM	Yes
Massachusetts	Republican	SBM	Yes
Michigan	Democrat	FFM	Yes
Minnesota	Democrat	SBM	Yes
Mississippi	Republican	FFM	No
Missouri	Republican	FFM	No
Montana	Democrat	FFM	Yes
Nebraska	Republican	FFM	Yes
Nevada	Democrat	SBM	Yes
New Hampshire	Republican	FFM	Yes
New Jersey	Democrat	SBM-FP	Yes
New Mexico	Democrat	SBM-FP	Yes
New York	Democrat	SBM	Yes
North Carolina	Democrat	FFM	No

North Dakota	Republican	FFM	Yes
Ohio	Republican	FFM	Yes
Oklahoma	Republican	FFM	No
Oregon	Democrat	SBM-FP	Yes
Pennsylvania	Democrat	SBM-FP	Yes
Rhode Island	Democrat	SBM	Yes
South Carolina	Republican	FFM	No
South Dakota	Republican	FFM	No
Tennessee	Republican	FFM	No
Texas	Republican	FFM	No
Utah	Republican	FFM	Yes
Vermont	Republican	SBM	Yes
Virginia	Democrat	FFM	Yes
Washington	Democrat	SBM	Yes
West Virginia	Republican	FFM	Yes
Wisconsin	Democrat	FFM	No
Wyoming	Republican	FFM	No

SBM: State-Based Marketplace;

SBM-FP: State-Based Marketplace - Federal Platform;

FFP: Federally-Facilitated Marketplace

Table 6.1: Medicaid Expansion Decisions by State
Source: Original Work
Attribution: Data Compiled Using Kaiser Family Foundation (KFF n.d.; KFF 2019) and state websites, table created by Keith Lee
License: CC BY-SA 4.0

The fourth provision, policy complexity, has been covered in the previous three factors. As you can see, there are many moving parts at various levels of government that rely on extensive oversight and coordination, both vertical and horizontal. The coordination dilemmas are largely managed by the Department of Health and Human Services (HHS). A report in 2012 by the Office of the Inspector General (a fixer) discussed the challenges with implementation. HHS worked as an intermediary between federal and state governments as well as coordinating the necessary federal agencies. Furthermore, according to the report, the "department would be forging new relationships with private insurers, providers, employers and consumers, all of whom will need clear information about benefits and responsibilities under ACA programs."

Lastly, the final two factors, incentives and resource allocation, work together in administering the program at the state level. The law required the federal government to pay for 100 percent of Medicaid expansion from 2014 to 2016 with a gradual drop from 2016 to 2020, when the government would continue paying 90% as long as the law was in place. Beyond state incentives and resource allocation, individuals were incentivized to buy into the program through the provisions below. The number in parentheses represents the percentage of people who think it is very important they be kept in place, according to a Kaiser Family Foundation Poll (Kirzinger, Muñana, and Brodie, 2019):

- Denying coverage for people with pre-existing conditions (72%).
- Denying coverage to pregnant women (71%).
- Prohibiting providers from charging sick people more (64%).
- Prohibiting lifetime limits (62%).
- Allowing young adults to stay on parents' insurance until age 26 (51%).

All-in-all, the ACA is a complex policy that still leads to heated debates in the halls of Congress and around tables at Thanksgiving. One of the many promises by Republicans during the 2016 election was to repeal and replace the Affordable Care Act. It has been three years, yet the law remains in place.

6.7 CRITICAL THINKING QUESTIONS – POLICY IMPLEMENTATION AND THE ACA

- How might implementation have been different if Republicans had been unsuccessful with their misinformation campaign?
- Look at your state's decision to expand Medicaid and find another state that made the opposite decision. How does each state differ post-expansion with regards to the number of individuals covered and the price of coverage?
- How might President Obama and the Democrats in Congress have improved their chances at implementation success?

6.8 CHAPTER SUMMARY

Policy implementation is a complex process that involves coordination between individuals, agencies, and policy makers. Managers, doers, and fixers are at the heart of the implementation process. Together they move the policy from a piece of legislation or executive order to something tangible. The implementation machinery, to borrow from Bardach, will produce policy at different speeds and with varying success rates based on the factors outlined above. Policy can have broad public support, originate from a favorable source, and have adequate resources secured but still stall prior to implementation if the administrative costs and burdens are too great. Similarly, a policy can be straightforward and require minimum effort for implementation yet never get passed if there is little political and/or public support. Thus, policy makers must continuously work the four primary levers to keep the machinery operational.

6.9 KEY TERMS

- Alternative Scenario Planning
- Bottom-Up Approach
- Design Levers
- Doers
- Fixers
- Horizontal Coordination
- Implementation
- Managers
- Operating System Levers
- Organizational Levers
- Political Levers
- Street-Level Bureaucrats
- Third Generation Approach
- Top-Down Approach
- Vertical Coordination

6.10 REFERENCES

Bardach, Eugene. 1977. The Implementation Game: What Happens When a Bill Becomes a Law. Cambridge, MA: The MIT Press.

Barr, Andy. 2010. "The GOP's No-Compromise Pledge." *Politico*, October 28, 2010. https://www.politico.com/story/2010/10/the-gops-no-compromise-pledge-044311

Birkland, Thomas A. 2019. An Introduction to the Policy Process: Theories, Concepts, and Models of Public Policy Making. New York: Routledge.

Brewer, Garry D. and Peter deLeon. 1983. The Foundations of Policy Analysis. Homewood, IL: The Dorsey Press.

Elmore, Richard.1985. "Forward and Backward Mapping." In Policy Implementation in Federal and Unitary Systems, eds. K. Hanf and T. Toonen, 33-70. Dordrecht: Martinus Nijhoff.

Goggin, Malcolm L., Ann O. Bowman, James P. Lester, and Lawrence J. O'Toole Jr. 1990. Implementation Theory and Practice: Toward a Third Generation. Glenview, IL: Scott, Foresman & Company, Little, Brown.

Jones, Charles O. 1984. An Introduction to the Study of Public Policy Monterey, CA: Brooks/Cole.

KFF. n.d. "State Health Insurance Market Place Types, 2020." *Kaiser Family Foundation*, n.d. https://www.kff.org/health-reform/state-indicator/state-health-

insurance-marketplace-types/?currentTimeframe=0&sortModel=%7B%22colId%22:
%22Location%22,%22sort%22:%22asc%22%7D

KFF. 2019. "Status of State Medicaid Expansion Decisions: Interactive Map." *Kaiser Family Foundation*, November 15, 2019. https://www.kff.org/medicaid/issue-brief/status-of-state-medicaid-expansion-decisions-interactive-map/

Kirzinger, Ashley, Cailey Muñana, and Mollyann Brodie. 2019. "6 Charts About Public Opinion on the Affordable Care Act." *Kaiser Family Foundation*, November 27, 2019. https://www.kff.org/health-reform/poll-finding/6-charts-about-public-opinion-on-the-affordable-care-act/

Kliff, Sarah. 2017. "Nancy Pelosi's One Obamacare Regret? Relying Too Much on Other Democrats for Messaging." *Vox*, January 12, 2017. https://www.vox.com/policy-and-politics/2017/1/12/14240014/pelosi-obamacare-repeal

Kraft, Michael E. and Scott R. Furlong. 2017. Public Policy: Politics, Analysis, and Alternatives. Thousand Oaks, CA: Sage/CQ Press.

Lipsky, Michael. 1980. Street Level Bureaucracy: Dilemmas of the Individual in Public Service. New York: Russel Sage Foundation.

Luft, Hal S. 1976. "Benefit-Cost Analysis and Public Policy Implementation," Public Policy 24, no. 4 (Fall): 450-451.

Nathan, Richard P. 1975. The Plot that Failed: Nixon and the Administrative Presidency. : John Wiley & Sons, Inc.

Office of Inspector General. 2012. "Management Issue 1: Implementing the Affordable Care Act." *Office of the Inspector General: U.S. Department of Health and Human Services*, n.d. https://www.kff.org/health-reform/poll-finding/6-charts-about-public-opinion-on-the-affordable-care-act/

Peters, Jeremy W. 2013. "Conservatives' Aggressive Ad Campaign Seeks to Cast Doubt on Health Law." *New York Times*, July 6, 2013. https://www.nytimes.com/2013/07/07/us/politics/conservatives-aggressive-ad-campaign-seeks-to-cast-doubt-on-health-law.html

Sabatier, Paul A. 1986. "Top-Down and Bottom-Up Approaches in Implementation Research: A Critical Analysis and Suggested Synthesis." Journal of Public Policy. 6 (1): 21-48.

Starling, Grover. 1988. Strategies for Policy Making. Chicago, IL: The Dorsey Press.

Theobald, Nick A. and Sean Nicholson-Crotty. "The Many Faces of Span of Control: Organizational Structure Across Multiple Goals." Administration and Society 36 (6): 648-660.

Weimer, David L and Aidan R. Vining. 2017. Policy Analysis: Concepts and Practice. New York: Routledge.

Policy Analysis and Evaluation

7.1 CHAPTER OBJECTIVES:

- Identify the differences between market and government failures.
- Recognize the steps in the policy analysis process.
- Apply each step to a real-world scenario.

Policy analysis is "client-oriented advice relevant to public decisions and informed by social values" (Weimer and Vining, 2017). Once they identify the root of the problem, analysts can begin the process of policy analysis which we discuss below. The methods we use here do not require economic modeling and are only meant to serve as an introduction to the process with the assumption that readers of the text understand the political process. Our approach builds upon the last chapter, which was grounded in the various tools policymakers have for policy implementation. Furthermore, it should be noted that, while the implementation chapter precedes the analysis chapter, both go together and are interchangeable. Policy analysis is, at some level, an ongoing process conducted throughout the policy process itself. In some cases, the alternatives considered during policy formulation may be rudimentary and used to gauge political feasibility and social acceptability.

7.2 THE POLICY ANALYSIS PROCESS

Now that we have discussed the reason policy analysis is needed, we can turn our attention to considering how to effectively conduct policy analysis. Scholars have proposed various processes; our process follows a similar path. The first step is identifying and defining the problem, which analysts use to effectively understand the problem's source and how they should specify the problem. The second step, identifying alternatives, is the process of identifying possible solutions for fixing the problem defined in step one. Next, establishing evaluation criteria determines how the analyst will decide on which alternative may best lead to success. Finally, the analyst selects the best alternative and then monitors it to ensure the desired outcomes are met.

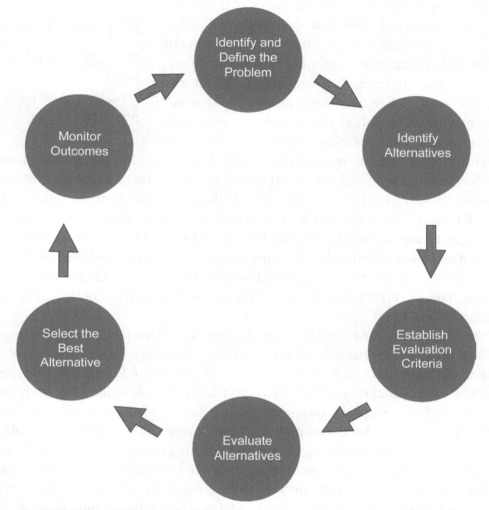

Figure 7.1: The Policy Analysis Cycle
Source: Original Work
Attribution: Keith Lee
License: CC BY-SA 4.0

7.3 IDENTIFY AND DEFINE THE PROBLEM

Patton, Sawicki, and Clark (2012) provide a useful framework for identifying and defining problems. The analyst must establish what is already known and assemble evidence that will be used to officially define the problem. At this point of the process, the problem may not be clearly defined and will likely include normative statements, such as "the rich should pay their fair share in taxes." The analyst will then need to operationalize what they mean by "rich" and "fair share." After identifying and defining the problem, analysts delineate the issue's boundaries in order to examine how long the problem has existed and in which context it has existed. Furthermore, analysts will consider in what ways this issue relates to other issues. Issue interconnectedness provides the analyst with a complex puzzle in which one piece's movement affects another piece's location.

Once the analyst knows which pieces of the puzzle must be considered, they can then begin collecting data and operationalizing terms based on gathered evidence. For example, they could now define "rich" as people making more than one billion dollars per year (or some other arbitrary cut point). This cut point may be set by polling that establishes an overall feeling of contempt for billionaires, thus making a policy targeting them more palatable. Similarly, defining the rich in this manner may be based on high end tax brackets that focus on raising taxes on this group in hopes of satisfying less affluent individuals by convincing them this solution is a "fair share." Once the fact base is established, the analyst can list goals and objectives to use gathered data and present it to affected parties to determine satisfaction/dissatisfaction levels of proposals to ascertain the likelihood of the policy success. While the primary audience will be the individuals asking for a change in policy, it is important that all parties be informed of how the policy will ultimately be defined.

> **Stop and Think**
>
> State a policy problem worth solving. How would you define the problem?

The analyst can now identify the policy envelope. This involves identifying all the data that must be considered when defining the policy. At this point, analysts have all the data they need, or at least think they need, and can begin displaying potential costs, benefits, and layouts in clear terms that describe what each party will gain and/or lose in the development of policy to rectify the policy problem. Once all steps have been completed, analysts can finally review the problem statement. This final step involves operationalizing ambiguous terms used in the first step that began the process. They could state the final problem statement as "individuals making over $250,000 are paying less in taxes than are those making less than $60,000, thus putting the burden on less affluent individuals." This problem statement is clear, specific, and concise.

7.4 IDENTIFY ALTERNATIVES

Alternatives refer to the various options an analyst can provide to their client. Alternatives from the previous example regarding the rich paying their fair share could be raising the marginal tax rates, raising the luxury tax, or imposing a greater inheritance tax. Similarly, maintaining the **status quo**, that is, not changing existing policy, is an alternative that must be considered. It is also worth stating, as Bardach and Patashnik (2020) note, that policy alternatives are not mutually exclusive. While one option may be to raise marginal tax rates and another may be to impose a luxury tax, these two potential choices can be combined for a third option: implementing both tax policies together. The analyst should then take all the proposed alternatives and compare them to the goals and objectives identified in the process so far. Once the final list has been narrowed to alternatives that are most likely to achieve the desired outcomes, the analyst should then present the list in a clear and concise manner.

A clear alternative is one that does not use policy jargon or long, complex ideas. Similarly, a concise alternative is written in a single sentence that captures the intent of the policy alternative, for example, raising the marginal tax rates on high earners. This is certainly clear and concise, but Bardach and Patashnik mention one final consideration: detail. As with the problem definition, the list of alternatives must be free of ambiguity. Therefore, a better statement would be to raise marginal tax rates by 17% on individuals making more than $750,000 per year.

> **Stop and Think**
>
> List two alternatives that you think would solve the policy problem you identified above.

How one develops the list of alternatives will heavily depend on the problem addressed, but a few tactics include studying existing scholarship and policy analyses, surveys, comparison of best practices and, depending on the experience level of the analyst, creative brainstorming. A review of the existing scholarship can be useful for all analysts but would likely benefit inexperienced analysts through fostering better understanding of the issue and creating additional exposure to research outlining problems and solutions with empirical evidence. Surveys may be useful to get a sense of feasibility and could also uncover audience expectations. Well written surveys with specified, open ended questions may provide the analyst with ideas they otherwise would not consider. Next, the comparative analysis technique allows analysts to examine what similar states, municipalities, or non-profits are doing, assuming they are facing or have faced similar problems. Analysts may look to these other areas as inspiration for what to propose, or study them in an effort to avoid alternatives that may not have produced the desired outcomes for such organizations. Lastly, analysts can use creative brainstorming to develop strategies that may not be routine or tested but could possibly solve the policy problem. As mentioned above, this tactic is one that would be used by a senior analyst familiar with the problem area.

7.5 ESTABLISH EVALUATION CRITERIA

A number of evaluation criteria have been suggested by scholars and practitioners (see Birkland, 2019; Kraft and Furlong, 2017; Patton, Sawicki, and Clark, 2012; Stone, 2012) from which we develop our criteria to consider: (1) effectiveness and efficiency, (2) equity and freedom, (3) political and administrative feasibility, and (4) social acceptability. The first of the listed criteria, effectiveness, can be used when alternatives utilize specific measures. For example, analysts working on alternatives to solve the previous problem of the rich not paying their fair share in taxes could develop several alternatives to solve the problem. Each alternative could then be analyzed for how useful the proposed solutions could be in solving the problem completely. One alternative to the problem we have defined is to raise the minimum wage. While this option does not directly impact all high earners, such a proposal could serve as a middle ground that may effectively close the income gap while appeasing low income workers. However, considering there are many salaried workers in the middle class, the solution may not satisfy the majority of less affluent individuals. Therefore, when compared to other proposed alternatives, this may be less effective. As we will see below, an alternatives matrix will allow us to compare this option to other possible alternatives based on the evaluation criteria.

Efficiency refers to the costs relative to the benefits after government intervention. Solving problems concerning the income gap are complex puzzles with many moving parts. While raising marginal tax rates on the rich and reducing tolls on those earning less than $60,000 may seem reasonable, other factors should be considered. One argument that top earners could make relates to the amount they contribute to charity foundations. Raising tax rates, they could argue, may reduce their contributions, thus negatively affecting their role in society. Similarly, considering the vast population difference between high and low earners, policies would have to be established to ensure the revenue lost by tax cuts is offset by the revenue generated by tax hikes.

Equity refers to equal outcomes among members of society. Arguments for and against tax hikes and cuts would likely revolve around equity. High earners could make the case that a uniform marginal tax rate is fair and equitable since everyone is treated the same. On the other hand, those on the low end of the income bracket may contest this claim because a larger portion, albeit the same percentage, is taken from them. An individual making $750,000 with a marginal tax rate set at 20% would have $600,000 after taxes. Conversely, an individual making $40,000 would be left with $32,000 after taxes. Once other costs are factored in, such as housing, clothing, and healthcare, the low-income individuals will have significantly less spending power. Consequently, fairness is not always equitable. Freedom, on the other hand, refers to an individual's right to pursue goals without interference. Therefore, in the example above, high earners can argue that, while the uniform tax cut may not be equitable, they have the freedom to earn without an excessive burden from the state. Hence, these two criteria are contradictory, but it is imperative that the analyst consider them both.

Political feasibility considers the acceptability of the policy by political stakeholders, such as those responsible for the legislation and execution of the policy. A policy alternative should not be selected if it is likely to die in the formulation process (see chapter 5). Similarly, administrative feasibility refers to the degree to which the policy can be successfully implemented (see chapter 6). Social acceptability considers the favorability of the policy proposal. Favorability can be gauged with political polling. Analysts considering social acceptability may also consider which adjustments, if any, they can make to a policy if the outcomes can be achieved, albeit with some concessions. For example, in the

2020 Democratic primary debates, there were a variety of proposals on the table regarding healthcare. The most extreme measure was Medicare for All, championed by Senator Bernie Sanders. Vice President Joe Biden, on the opposite end of the spectrum, was in favor of incremental changes to the Affordable Care Act. Candidates in between the two proposed a middle ground plan, often referred to by Mayor Pete Buttigieg as Medicare for all who want it. This proposal would offer a public option while keeping private insurers in the market. According to a Marist poll (Marist Poll), in the summer of 2019—just as the Democratic primary got into full swing—70% of those polled favored Medicare for all who want it (90% of Democrats, 46% of Republicans, and 70% of Independents) compared to only 41% favorability for Medicare for all (64% of Democrats, 14% of Republicans, and 39% of Independents).

7.6 EVALUATE THE ALTERNATIVES

The next step, now that you have identified the alternatives and established the evaluation criteria you will use, is to evaluate the alternatives you selected above. An alternative matrix is a useful tool for comparing alternatives side-by-side. Table 7.1 below provides an example of an alternative matrix based on the problem defined earlier. Once you fill in the matrix, you can analyze each column to determine the favored policy for each criterion. From there, you can determine the preferred alternative. However, one thing worth considering is how each evaluation criterion is weighted. Political feasibility may need to be weighted more if it is an election year, for example. One technique analysts use to evaluate alternatives is implementation analysis. Implementation analysis, according to Steiss and Daneke (1980), involves examining the policy in terms of feasibility. They contend two metrics to consider when forecasting feasibility are "magnitude of change" and "degree of consensus." Degree of consensus revolves around the popularity, per se, of the proposed alternative. The magnitude of change is what it sounds like: how much different is this proposal from the status quo. Both of these concepts relate to the evaluation criteria mentioned above, but it may be helpful to look at them as they relate to each other. Alternatives with high consensus and low magnitude of change will be easier to implement than those with a high magnitude of change and low consensus.

Stop and Think

Create your own matrix like Table 7.1. Evaluate the alternatives you listed above along with the status quo. Which one is the best alternative based on the evaluation criteria you selected?

Criteria Alternative	Effectiveness	Efficiency	Equity	Freedom	Political Feasibility	Admin Feasibility	Social Acceptance	Total Checkmarks
Status Quo								
Raise Marginal Tax Rates on everyone by X%								
Increase tax rates on high income by X% and cut taxes by X% on middle/low income								
Favored Option								

Table 7.1: Alternative Matrix for Tax Cuts Example
Source: Original Work
Attribution: Keith Lee
License: CC BY-SA 4.0

7.7 SELECT THE BEST ALTERNATIVE AND MONITOR OUTCOMES

You can now present the preferred outcome to the client. Assuming the policy is accepted and proposed, it will now begin the formulation stage (see chapter 5). Once the policy is formed, it can move into the implementation stage (see chapter 6). Finally, once the policy is fully implemented, policymakers can monitor it based on the expected outcomes. Future analysis may need to be conducted if the policy does not adequately solve the problem identified in step one, in which case it goes through the policy analysis process again. Policy problems are rarely solved on the first try, as we discuss in the running case study that has been presented throughout the book. Societal and political shifts will change over time, thus negating policies that successfully achieved the designed outcomes. Therefore, policymakers and analysts must continuously monitor the political climate in order to reduce the recognition gap. Policy analysis, as we have shown, is a complicated and complex endeavor.

The process now returns to the evaluation stage after the selected policy is adopted to determine if the outcomes are met. Policies are monitored to assess their success as determined by whether the strategies achieved their desired outcomes. Policy failure can occur programmatically and/or theoretically (Weiss, 1972). Program failure occurs when a policy is not implemented as designed. Theoretical failure happens when a program is implemented as designed but does not deliver desired results. Obamacare, for example, suffered from both failures. As noted in the chapter 6 case study, states won a critical battle upending the designed implementation (program failure), and the policy, once implemented, failed to provide the desired results (theoretical failure), which we discuss in the case study below. However, in this case, the theoretical failure could be a result of the program failure; that is, had states implemented the policy as designed, the desired results would have followed. Analysts can use a variety of methods to assess policy outcomes. We outline four below and recommend *Basic Methods of Policy Analysis and Planning* (Patton, Sawicki, and Clark, 2012) to students wishing to dive deeper into analysis methods.

Before and after comparisons determine the success of policy outputs by examining the policy effects directly. For example, a state decides to implement a policy lowering the speed limit to 55 miles per hour on the interstate to minimize traffic fatalities. The analyst could compare the number of fatalities during a specific time period before the intervention and in the years after the policy was enacted. However, one thing to consider when conducting before and after comparisons are external factors that may contribute to the policy output. Consider, for example, vehicle safety ratings. The reduction in fatalities may have been lowered if car manufacturers began shipping out safer cars at the same time as the new policy being implemented. Therefore, analysts may want to consider with or without comparisons if external factors might affect the results.

With or without comparisons take into account two or more cases in which at least one of the cases did not receive treatment. In the example above, the analyst could compare one state to another if the other state did not change its speed limit law. Georgia, for example, could lower the speed limit and then compare their fatality numbers to Alabama. This study would offset any effect generated by safer vehicle manufacturing, though it does have a weakness that analysts may need to consider. When selecting cases, it is imperative that analysts choose locales that are similar (geographically and demographically). Georgia and Alabama, while both neighboring southern states, are different geographically. Roughly 50% of Georgia's population resides in the metro Atlanta area. Alabama does not have a similar metro area. As such, the analyst may want to analyze fatalities just outside of the metro area.

Experimental models go beyond the previous two methods by controlling the environment completely whereby the only change on the treatment group is the actual treatment. Unfortunately, these models are rarely possible outside of the hard sciences (e.g., biology), so researchers must rely on **quasi-experimental models**. These models control as much of the environment as possible to eliminate as many external factors as possible. These models are better suited on small scale policies, such as those implemented at the local level.

All in all, the method selected will largely be determined by the size and scope of the policy. As mentioned, quasi-experimental models are best suited for small scale policies due to the necessary controls that must be included. Before and after comparisons, on the other hand, may be the only method available for large scale scenarios. For example, analyzing the Affordable Care Act would not be possible if using the with or without methods, as it would not be possible to compare the policy to a non-treatment case.

7.8 CASE STUDY: ANALYZING THE AFFORDABLE CARE ACT

Republicans in Congress have yet to repeal and replace the Affordable Care Act, even though such vows have been mainstays in Republican campaigns since the law's passage in 2010. Furthermore, Republicans controlled both chambers of Congress and the White House from 2017 to 2019. Why, then, were they unable to get the policy repealed and replaced with a better option? The policy analysis process may help us understand why repeal is unlikely. We can begin the analysis process now that we have identified the root cause of the problem. However, we use the post-2016 election as a starting point rather than looking back and analyzing the status quo prior to the ACA with the ACA as an alternative. Instead, Obamacare will be the status quo and we will examine alternatives to improve upon Obamacare. What follows is a rudimentary example of how one might analyze a policy and propose an alternative.

7.8.1 Identify and Define the Problem

Obamacare had three goals (Healthcare.gov):

1. Make affordable insurance available to everyone.

2. Expand the Medicaid program.

3. Support innovative programs.

Obamacare has failed to meet its goals. Insurance is not affordable to everyone and remains too expensive in some states where premiums continue to climb (Goodnough, 2019). Similarly, the Medicaid expansion requirement was unsuccessful due to legal constraints that allowed states the opportunity to opt out of the expansion requirement. Examining the third goal is beyond the scope of this study, as it would require defining and identifying "innovative programs." Given these shortcomings, we define the problem as follows:

> 27.4 million non-elderly individuals in the U.S. remain uninsured in 2017. 45% of those uninsured report cost as the reason, particularly among low-income families with at least one worker in the household (KFF, 2018).

7.8.2 Identify Alternatives

We use four alternatives analyzed by the RAND corporation (RAND).

- Maintain the ACA with no changes (the status quo).
- Repeal the ACA with no replacement.
- Repeal the ACA with single payer plan (e.g., Medicare for All).
- Replace with another option.

7.8.3 Select Evaluation Criteria

We will use all the criteria listed above except for efficiency. Efficiency would require a deeper look at each alternative that is beyond the scope of the case study, but suffice it to say that the analyst would begin by looking at costs and comparing them to the benefits. In this case, some benefits, such as the enhancement of positive externalities, would be difficult to quantify. Therefore, rather than attempting to analyze the efficiency of the policies, which could require journal article length studies, we will simply use effectiveness. Effectiveness will be determined by the number of people expected to be covered by each policy, with the most effective policy being 100% coverage. Equity will be compared by determining the expected cost and benefit for each individual. Much like efficiency, equity would need a large-scale study to fully analyze how equitable each policy is, but we use a simplified approach of comparing individual costs to benefits. Freedom, on the other hand, will be measured by the ability to choose your own insurance plan. Political feasibility is simply the likelihood that the policy can be passed in Congress and signed into law by the president. Lastly, we will consider social acceptability by comparing public polling. Outright repeal is measured with a poll from the Kaiser Family Foundation in 2019 that asked respondents if they wanted the Supreme Court to overturn the ACA. Our other option of replacing the ACA with a single payer plan will use Medicare for All polling as its social acceptability measurement.

Evaluate Alternatives

We will now list each policy and evaluate them independently rather than beginning with a matrix. We will then put a check mark in the matrix for the best policy based on each criterion to give an overview of how they compare. Lastly, we will total the checkmarks and put forth our policy proposal.

Maintaining the ACA with no changes (the status quo).

- Effectiveness: 27.4 million people are not covered.
- Equity: Everyone has access to coverage, but some remain unable to afford it.
- Freedom: Individuals choose their provider and their plan, but everyone is mandated to have coverage, which limits individual freedom.
- Political Feasibility: The policy is already in place.
- Administrative Feasibility: The policy is currently implemented and administered, thus the administrative costs will be unchanged if a new policy plan cannot be reached.
- Social Acceptability: 51% approve (Kirzinger, Muñana, and Brodie, 2019).

Repeal the ACA with no replacement.

- Effectiveness: Number of uninsured would likely return to pre-2010 levels which would be less effective than the ACA.
- Equity: Everyone has access but fewer people will be able to afford it.
- Freedom: Individuals are free to decide on coverage as well as if they want coverage at all.
- Political Feasibility: Unlikely to pass considering the overall favorability of individual provisions within the law.
- Administrative Feasibility: It is feasible that the rollback could occur administratively.
- Social Acceptability: 52% want the Supreme Court to overturn the ACA, even though 56% of respondents worry that they or someone in their family will lose coverage (Kirzinger, Muñana, and Brodie, 2019).

Repeal the ACA with Single Payer.

- Effectiveness: Everyone is covered.
- Equity: Everyone will be able to afford coverage, though higher earners will be taxed more.
- Freedom: There will not be any choice in provider.
- Political Feasibility: Unlikely to pass.
- Administrative Feasibility: Would build off the current system.
- Social Acceptability: 51% (Lopes et al., 2019).

Repeal the ACA with Other Proposals.

- Effectiveness: Will depend on specific proposal but would likely cover fewer people based on analysis conducted by RAND.
- Equity: Everyone has access but there is not a guarantee it would be more affordable.
- Freedom: Everyone will be able to choose if they want coverage and which coverage they prefer.
- Political Feasibility: Unlikely to pass based on 2017 results.
- Administrative Feasibility: Feasible considering most proposals according to RAND vary slightly and keep many of the provisions in place.
- Social Acceptability: no current data.

7.8.4 Alternatives Matrix

Criteria / Alternative	Most Effective	Equity	Freedom	Political Feasibility	Admin Feasibility	Social Acceptance	Total Checkmarks
ACA as is (status quo)				✓		✓	2
Repeal ACA, no replacement			✓				1
Replace ACA with Single Payer	✓					✓	2
Replace ACA with other option							0
Preferred Alternative	Status Quo or Medicare for All						

Table 7.2: Alternatives Matrix for ACA Case Study
Source: Original Work
Attribution: Keith Lee
License: CC BY-SA 4.0

7.8.5 Select Preferred Alternative

The preferred outcome will be maintaining the ACA or replacing it with Medicare for All. Note that equity and administrative feasibility did not have a clear winner. The decision to select an alternative would rest with how each criterion is weighted. Political feasibility, considering the policy process that we have outlined in this book, is likely to be weighted higher. However, this weighing has the potential to change in the next decade. Given the current political climate and divided government, it is unlikely that the ACA will be repealed. Similarly, the law will likely remain in place post-2020 unless Democrats win a majority in the House, a super majority in the Senate, put Senator Sanders in the White House, and receive overwhelming support for Medicare for All by the people.

7.9 CRITICAL THINKING QUESTIONS – POLICY ANALYSIS AND THE ACA

- Why have Republicans been unable to successfully repeal the ACA?
- Pick one repeal and replace the option proposed by Republicans. Create an alternatives matrix like the one above and compare it to the status quo. Would it be the preferred option?
- Draft a proposal for healthcare policy that would be the best option for each of the criteria above. Which criterion is easiest to satisfy? Which one is the most difficult?

7.10 CHAPTER SUMMARY

Policy analysis has two major components. The first is diagnosing the problem to determine its source, e.g., government or market failure. The second component is the actual analysis stage. This stage can be completed in a variety of ways, but we have outlined one above that draws from a number of sources. The key to good policy analysis is to recognize and consider all alternatives rather than those that will satisfy the client. Similarly, the analyst must choose selection criteria that will not unfairly advantage one alternative over another. Lastly, the analyst should carefully compose a memo to the client outlining the process used to select the preferred alternative. After receiving the memo, the policy maker will see that the new policy gets implemented by returning to the steps outlined in the previous chapter.

7.11 KEY TERMS
- Experimental Models
- Policy Analysis
- Quasi-experimental models
- Status Quo

7.12 REFERENCES

Bardach, Eugene and Eric M. Patashnik. 2020. A Practical Guide for Policy Analysis: The Eightfold Path to More Effective Problem Solving. Thousand Oaks, CA: CQ Press.

Goodnough, Abby. 2019. "Obamacare Premiums to Fall and Number of Insurers to Rise Next Year." *New York Times*, October 22, 2019. https://www.nytimes.com/2019/10/22/us/politics/obamacare-trump.html

Gupta, Dipak K. 2011. Analyzing Public Policy: Concepts, Tools, and Techniques. Washington, DC: CQ Press.

Healthcare.gov. n.d. "Affordable Care Act." https://www.healthcare.gov/glossary/affordable-care-act/

Hill, Holly A., Laurie D. Elam-Evans, David Yankey, James Singleton, Yoonjae Kang. 2018. "Vaccination Coverage Among Children Aged 19 – 35 Months – United States, 2017." *Centers for Disease Control: Morbidity and Mortality Weekly Report*, October 12, 2018. https://www.cdc.gov/mmwr/volumes/67/wr/mm6740a4.htm

KFF. 2017. "Compare Proposals to Replace the Affordable Care Act." *Kaiser Family Foundation*, September 18, 2017. https://www.kff.org/interactive/proposals-to-replace-the-affordable-care-act/

KFF. 2018. "Key Facts About the Uninsured Population." *Kaiser Family Foundation*, December 7, 2018. https://www.kff.org/uninsured/fact-sheet/key-facts-about-the-uninsured-population/

Kirzinger, Ashley, Cailey Muñana, and Mollyann Brodie. 2019. "6 Charts About Public Opinion on the Affordable Care Act." *Kaiser Family Foundation*, November 27, 2019. https://www.kff.org/health-reform/poll-finding/6-charts-about-public-opinion-on-the-affordable-care-act/

Lopes, Lunna, Liz Hamel, Audrey Kearney, and Mollyann Brodie. 2019. "KFF Tracking-Poll – October 2019: Health Care in the Democratic Debates, Congress, and the Courts." *Kaiser Family Foundation*, October 15, 2019. https://www.kff.org/health-reform/poll-finding/kff-health-tracking-poll-october-2019/

Patton, Carl V., David Sawicki and Jennifer Clark. 2012. Basic Methods of Policy Analysis and Planning. New York, NY: Routledge.

RAND. n.d. "The Future of U.S. Health Care: Replace or Revise the Affordable Care Act?" https://www.rand.org/health-care/key-topics/health-policy/in-depth.html

Stone, Deborah. 2012. Policy Paradox: The Art of Political Decision Making. New York, NY: W.W. Norton & Company

Printed in the USA
CPSIA information can be obtained
at www.ICGtesting.com
LVHW071238051223
765561LV00010B/766